NUBIA

LOST CIVILIZATIONS

The books in this series explore the rise and fall of the great civilizations and peoples of the ancient world. Each book considers not only their history but their art, culture and lasting legacy and asks why they remain important and relevant in our world today.

Already published:

The Aztecs Frances F. Berdan
The Barbarians Peter Bogucki
Egypt Christina Riggs
The Etruscans Lucy Shipley
The Goths David M. Gwynn
The Greeks Philip Matyszak
The Inca Kevin Lane
The Indus Andrew Robinson
The Maya Megan E. O'Neil
Nubia Sarah M. Schellinger
The Persians Geoffrey Parker and Brenda Parker
The Phoenicians Vadim S. Jigoulov
The Sumerians Paul Collins

NUBIA
LOST CIVILIZATIONS

SARAH M. SCHELLINGER

REAKTION BOOKS

For Mom and Dad

Published by Reaktion Books Ltd
Unit 32, Waterside
44–48 Wharf Road
London N1 7UX, UK
www.reaktionbooks.co.uk

First published 2022
Copyright © Sarah M. Schellinger 2022

Printed and bound in India by Replika Press Pvt. Ltd

A catalogue record for this book is available from the British Library

ISBN 978 1 78914 659 2

CHRONOLOGY

c. 1,000,000–10,000 BP	Palaeolithic period: stone tools used for hunting, gathering and fishing
c. 8000–5000 BC	Mesolithic period: seasonal, semi-sedentary camps
c. 4900–3000 BC	Neolithic period: beginnings of animal husbandry and farming
c. 3800–2900 BC	A-Group: increase in social stratification
c. 24/2300–1600 BC	C-Group: documented Egyptian Old Kingdom expeditions to Nubia
c. 3000–2500 BC	Pre-Kerma period
c. 2500–1450 BC	Kerma period: first Nubian capital and kingdom
c. 2055–1650 BC	Construction of Egyptian Middle Kingdom fortresses to control riverine traffic between Egypt and Nubia

c. 1550–1070 BC	Egyptian New Kingdom colonization of Nubia
c. 1070–800 BC	Nubian 'dark age': evidence of lavish burials at Hillat el-Arab
c. 800–300 BC	Napatan period in Nubia: pyramid construction begins at royal cemetery of el-Kurru; possible reign of Queen Katimalo
c. 760–747 BC	Reign of Kashta, first Nubian ruler to attempt conquest of Egypt; installation of his daughter Amenirdis I as God's Wife of Amun in Thebes
c. 728 BC	Piye begins his second march north and defeats Egyptian rebels; documents conquest on his Great Triumphal Stela; installation of his daughter Shepenwepet II as God's Wife of Amun
c. 716 BC	Shabaqo crowned at Memphis, marking official beginning of Nubian rule in Egypt, known as Dynasty 25
690–664 BC	Reign of Taharqo; movement of royal burial grounds from el-Kurru to Nuri; his daughter Amenirdis II serves as last Nubian God's Wife of Amun
c. 664–656 BC	Reign of Tanwetamani; ousting of Nubians by Assyrian invasion of Egypt led by Assurbanipal
Last 3rd of 4th century BC	Possible reign of Queen Sakhmakh, widow of King Nastaseñ

c. 300 BC–AD 350	Meroitic period: capital moved from Napata to Meroe; advent of Nubian ironworking
c. 270–260 BC	Burial of King Arkamani in South Cemetery at Meroe
Late 3rd century BC	Royal burial ground moved from South to North Cemetery at Meroe by King Amanitikha
2nd century BC	First appearance of Meroitic writing system
Last 3rd of 1st century BC	Reign of Queen Amanirenas; defeat of Roman army and capture of bronze head of Augustus (now in the British Museum)
21 BC	Treaty of Samos between Rome and Meroe
AD 253	King Teqorideamani ends reign as last dated Meroitic ruler
Mid-4th century AD	Invasion of Meroe by Ezana, first Christian king of Aksum, and fall of Meroitic Empire
c. 350–550	Post-Meroitic period: rise of kingdoms at Nobadia, Makuria and Alwa
Late 4th or early 5th century	Inscription of Kharamadoye on Temple of Mandulis at Kalabsha, last known Meroitic inscription
Mid-6th century	Christianization of Nubia

652	Baqt treaty between Christian Nubia and Muslim Egypt
8th century	Nobadia and Makuria united under one ruler
16th century	Rise of Funj Sultanate and Islamization of Nubia
1821	Muhammad Ali conquers Sudan in the name of the Ottoman Empire
1881–98	Mahdist State
1884	Siege of Khartoum
1899–1913	Anglo-Egyptian Sudan: Herbert Kitchener appointed first governor-general in 1899
1956	Sudan independence from Anglo-Egyptian rule
1971	Sudan National Museum established in Khartoum
1985	Removal of Jaafar Nimeiri
2011	Referendum vote and recognition of the Republic of South Sudan
2018–19	Protests in Khartoum; Alaa Salah dubbed 'Kandaka' and becomes face of revolution; arrest of Omar al-Bashir on 17 April and removal from presidential palace

2021   Military coup led by General Abdel Fattah al-Burhan on 25 October in an attempt to overthrow the transitional government; the civilian prime minister, Abdalla Hamdok, placed under house arrest; Abdalla Hamdok reinstated as prime minister on 21 November and political prisoners freed

2022   Abdalla Hamdok resigns as prime minister on 2 January

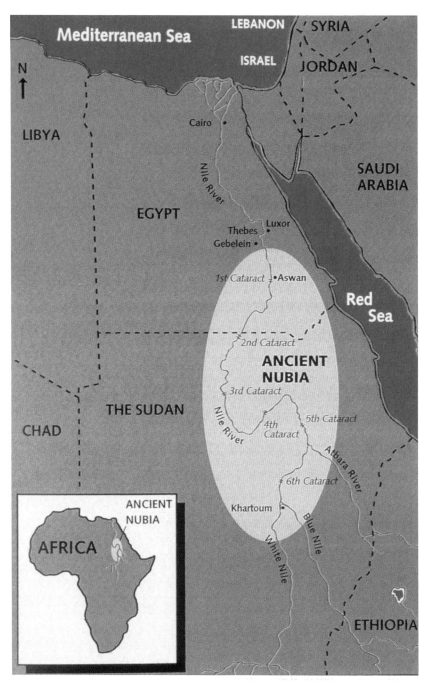

Modern-day northeast Africa, and the location of ancient Nubia within it.

ONE

THE 'LOST' LAND OF NUBIA

W hen thinking about the ancient world, Mesopotamia, Egypt, Greece and Rome come to mind. However, one of the most common misconceptions is that Egypt was isolated and not one of many thriving cultures that developed in northeastern Africa prior to the Arabization of the region beginning in the seventh century AD. To this end, Nubia (modern-day southernmost Egypt and North Sudan) has historically been viewed through the eyes of ancient Egypt as well as early European and American travellers and archaeologists. This skewed vantage point makes Nubia an ideal addition to the 'Lost Civilizations' series, because in many ways Nubia has indeed been 'lost' and forgotten as a society that helped develop and build the region of northeastern Africa into an ancient world power.

By our modern standards, a world power is a country that has influence over foreign affairs and, by extension, peoples. This influence could be seen as positive or negative depending on the viewpoint, a concept as familiar to the ancients as it is to us now. Although the areas incorporated into the ancients' idea of what their world encompassed was smaller than what we consider today, during the period referred to as the Egyptian Twenty-Fifth Dynasty, the Nubians controlled an area from at least the Fourth Cataract in the south to the Delta in the north. They monitored the flow of people throughout their empire, fashioned themselves as the rightful rulers of the Double Kingdom, and participated in long-distance trade with their neighbours throughout the Mediterranean, southwest Asia and along the Red Sea.

Should Nubia be considered 'lost' when the land still exists and there are many descendants of these ancient peoples? Yes, because while Egypt has been viewed as a pinnacle of ancient civilization for decades, many early explorers and archaeologists considered Nubia to be less than its northern counterpart. One of the reasons for this belief is that the Nubians did not have a written language prior to the colonization of the country by the ancient Egyptians during the New Kingdom (*c*. 1550–1070 BC). Although they obviously had verbal communication, they had not developed a writing system, so could not tell us about their history in their own words. With the lack of written documents prior to the New Kingdom colonization, we must rely on the archaeological evidence, which primarily comes from religious and funerary contexts. This has slanted information in favour of the ruling and elite classes, with less known about the non-ruling and non-elite members of society. Even when written language is introduced, all of the documents are restricted to the literate members of society, therefore leaving us without the voices of the bulk of the Nubian population.

Despite the lack of writing, we see testaments to higher thinking and ingenuity without the need for modern power tools or engineering degrees. From the temples and palaces to the tomb structures, we see not only the adaptation of foreign archetypes but the resonance of indigenous Nubian processes. Now more than ever, we can see the power and might of an ancient society that, despite not developing their own writing system until rather late in the game, created a civilization that was not 'lost' but rather contextualized under the framework of another powerful African civilization: the ancient Egyptians.

Whether considering the Nubians from the perspective of the Egyptians or the early travellers to the area, we cannot help but notice their biases against the Nubians and their collective disregard for Nubian culture. Even early archaeologists, when confronted with the evidence of contact with Egypt, assumed they were looking at proof of Egyptian power rather than considering that the Egyptians had been overcome by their southern neighbours. The aim of this book is to bring Nubia out of the shadow of

Egypt and place it at the forefront as an ancient world power that is certainly not, nor really ever has been, 'lost'.

Geography and environment

The terms 'Nubia' and 'Nubians' might have derived from the Egyptian word for gold (*nebu*). Nubia was an area rich in gold, which was extensively mined, and coveted, by the ancient Egyptians. However, the ancient Egyptians did not use the word 'Nubia' to refer to their southern neighbour. Instead they used the term *Ta-sety*, meaning 'Land of the Bow', because the Nubians were expert archers who often served in the Egyptian military. In addition to referring to Nubia as the 'Land of the Bow', the Middle Kingdom Egyptians started referring to it as 'Kush' or, when they wanted to vilify their southern neighbours, 'wretched Kush'. The term 'Kushite' has been adopted to refer to the collective timeframe of the Napatan (*c.* 800–300 BC) and Meroitic (*c.* 300 BC–AD 350) periods when Nubia was a ruling power in its own right. Classical writers referred to the country as 'Ethiopia/Aithiopia', meaning 'burnt face' in Greek, as a reference to the dark-skinned inhabitants of northeastern Africa. However, this term is archaic, inaccurate and was never used by the Egyptians or the Nubians.

Today, Nubia is located in present-day North Sudan and the southern part of Egypt. In antiquity it was the country that ranged from roughly the Sixth Cataract in the south to the First Cataract in the north, which was the ancient boundary between Nubia and Egypt. It was the country where the White Nile from Lake Victoria in present-day Kenya, Uganda and Tanzania and the Blue Nile from Lake Tana in present-day Ethiopia converged at Khartoum, the capital of North Sudan, to form the Nile River, which flowed for about 2,730 kilometres (1,696 mi.) to the Mediterranean Sea. The actual confines of the country were from the Nile Confluence in Khartoum to just north of Aswan (Jebel el-Silsileh), an area spanning approximately 1,450 kilometres (900 mi.).

Unlike in Egypt, the Nile did not flow smoothly but rather was interrupted by six cataracts, rocky granite outcroppings, which

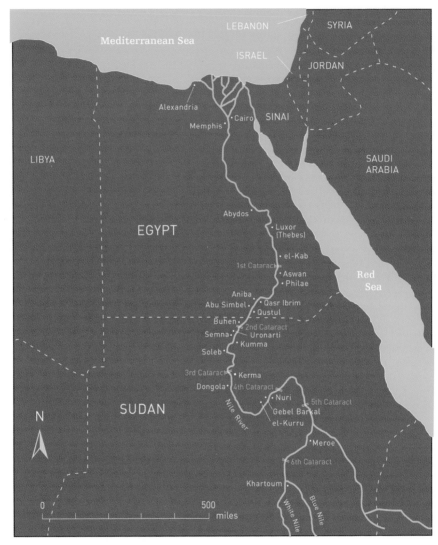

The significant sites of Nubia in present-day Egypt and Sudan.

First Cataract rapids, 1877.

prevent travel by boat in these areas. Because of the cataracts, boats had to be removed from the water and carried through the desert until the travellers reached the opposite side of the rapids. This created many desert routes throughout the country that served as primary means of transporting people and goods.

The Nubian landscape, in contrast to Egypt, was much drier and did not have the same large-scale irrigation systems that supported an agriculture-based economic system. The range of climatic areas and the susceptibility of the northern and central regions to minor temperature and rainfall variations would have impacted the stability of the agricultural and pastoral potential in Nubia. Most settlements were located adjacent to the Nile in order to utilize the annual flood in preparing the fields for cultivation. Irrigation was aided with the adoption of the *saqia* waterwheel in the late Meroitic and Post-Meroitic periods (*c.* AD 350–550). This allowed for year-round cultivation and agricultural expansion into previously uninhabitable places.

Nubia was not isolated, but interacted with its neighbours. To the north was Egypt. Contact between the two countries spanned their respective histories and highlights their longstanding friendship and rivalry. To the west was the desert region allowing movement along the Wadi Howar to the Darfur area. To the east was the Aksumite Empire, encompassing modern-day Ethiopia and Eritrea. Evidence for trade relations between Nubia and Aksum can be found from at least the Kerma period (c. 2500 BC–AD 350). Also located somewhere in this area is the enigmatic land of Punt. Trade between Egypt and Punt is particularly evident at the Middle Kingdom Red Sea port site of Mersa Gawasis and most famously on the walls of the New Kingdom Mortuary Temple of Hatshepsut at Deir el-Bahri. The exact location of Punt remains uncertain, but was probably along the eastern coast of the Horn of Africa because the area was accessible from the Red Sea and the products returning to Egypt had an African rather than Yemeni point of origin.

Toponyms

Nubian place names and their locations have been the topic of extensive research within Egyptology and Nubian studies. The earliest records that provide us with this information come from the autobiographies of Egyptian nobles who travelled to Nubia during the Old Kingdom. However, it is apparent that they were more concerned with detailing the items they brought back to Egypt than the exact locations from where the objects were acquired.

Within Nubia there are two primary regions, Lower Nubia, located between the First and Second Cataracts, and Upper Nubia, spanning from the Second to Sixth Cataracts. In antiquity Lower Nubia was generally referred to as Wawat and Upper Nubia as Kush. Lower Nubia was further subdivided into three regions: Wawat was the northernmost of these regions and was located from Elephantine to the Dakka region. Irtjet was located to the south of Wawat, beginning at the Dakka region and ending at Toshka, just north of Buhen. The third region was known as Setju and was located to the south of Irtjet, beginning at Toshka and ending at the Second Cataract. Evidence of Irtjet can be found on a graffito in the Tomas area carved by someone on an expedition sent by Pepy I (*c.* 2321–2287 BC) to 'open up or explore' Irtjet. Even with the graffito, it is unclear as to whether Tomas was in Irtjet or on the way to Irtjet.

One of the other important sites is that of Yam. It has been considered to be the southernmost location of interest to the Egyptians. References to Yam are first attested in Old Kingdom texts, where it refers to a southern region, linked to other known southern regions listed in the *Autobiography of Harkhuf*. Interestingly, Yam is not mentioned in inscriptions aside from topographical lists after the early Middle Kingdom. Several locations have been proposed for the location of Yam: the Shendi Reach of Upper Nubia between the Fifth and Sixth Cataracts, where the Atbara River flows into the Nile River; Upper Nubia, possibly as a part of Kerma; southwest of Aswan at the Dunkul Oasis; probably not south of the 22nd parallel, thereby placing Yam outside of Upper Nubia; somewhere in the Western Desert near Jebel Uweinat or Ennedi.[1]

Many of these place names can be connected to Egyptian words. For example, *irtjet* means 'milk' in Egyptian, *setju* means 'ground' or 'libation stone', and *mekher* means 'silo' or 'low-lying land'.[2] It remains unclear whether the Egyptians were designating areas based on their own geographical terminology or whether they were trying to equate Nubian names with their closest approximations.[3]

Topographical lists contained more than two hundred location names, yet their exact locations remain unclear, since toponyms continued to evolve throughout Nubian history. When the Middle Kingdom fortresses were built in the Second Cataract region and the temple towns were founded during New Kingdom colonization, Egyptian names were attached to the buildings to reflect the might of Egypt, as well as to pay homage to the king who commissioned them.

Natural resources

Nubia was a land rich in natural resources that were highly coveted by its neighbours, particularly the ancient Egyptians. Gold was one of the most valued materials from Nubia and the Egyptians did everything in their power to gain and keep control of the mines there. Gold was used to make jewellery, cast statues of deities and embellish furniture.

The tribute scene from the tomb of Amenhotep, called Huy, highlights that Nubian gold and gold mining was a lucrative facet of the economy. The richest gold deposits are located in the Eastern Desert region near Aniba and the Wadi Allaqi. New Kingdom gold mining in Nubia is almost exclusively restricted to the time from Thutmose III (*c*. 1479–1425 BC) to Akhenaten (*c*. 1352–1336 BC), after which there is no more evidence of pharaonic gold mining south of the Wadi Allaqi. However, gold mining continued in the Eastern Desert of Egypt until the end of the Ramesside period (*c*. 1295–1070 BC).[4] Gold mining in the Abri-Delgo Reach from the reign of Amenhotep III (*c*. 1390–1352 BC) to the Ramesside period probably began as the gold supply in the Eastern Desert dwindled and new gold sources were being exploited from the Third Cataract region.

Animals were integral to the Nubian lifestyle. Rock drawings found throughout the country include a multitude of wild animal images, including giraffes, oryx, gazelles, hartebeest, donkeys, elephants, hippopotami, rhinoceroses, ostriches and hares. Nubians used elephant and hippopotamus ivory to make decorative items and jewellery, especially from the Kerma period onwards. Like gold, it was also used to make jewellery, headrests, small statues and decorative inlays for furniture. Ivory bracelets were also commonly worn during the Old Kingdom.

The Nubians participated in raising large herds of cattle not only for dairy and meat, but for the production of leather products that included sandals, belts, quivers, bags and harnesses. The southern provinces were primarily exporters of raw materials and animals, and were importers of manufactured goods. During the Graeco-Roman period in Egypt there was increased travel to

Nubia, partly to obtain war elephants from Meroe. The Nubians possibly also used elephants for warfare, as seen in the many representations of elephants and conquered foes from the Great Enclosure at Musawwarat es-Sufra. At one time it was suggested that the site had been used as a training ground for the elephants, but this has since been disproven. In exchange for the elephants, the Meroitic rulers received luxury items such as silver, bronze and glass. The use of trade as a primary component of the Meroitic economy can also be seen by the placement of Meroe, Napata and Kawa. These sites were located at the terminal points of the major overland desert routes: the Bayuda Road, the Meheila Road and the Korosko Road.[5] Competition for control of these routes may have led to the conflict between Nubia and Aksum, who each vied for dominance over the raw materials required for export upon which both empires depended.

Elephant statue at Musawwarat es-Sufra.

War elephants and raw materials were not the only items traded with the Graeco-Roman world. Some scholars have proposed that the Meroitic rulers also engaged in the trading of slaves.[6] The Egyptian pharaohs openly boasted about the number of Nubian captives they brought back from their southern campaigns, which may in actuality have been slave raids. The presence of Black people in Ptolemaic Alexandria was not considered an unusual sight since these individuals may have been introduced as slaves or prisoners of war. Potential evidence for the slave trade has been linked to the presence of living rather than dead prisoners on the pylons of the Lion Temple at Naqa, as well as the association of captives and elephants on the interior walls of the Lion Temple at Musawwarat es-Sufra. All of these reliefs show bound prisoners – in a manner similar to representations of bound prisoners in ancient Egyptian reliefs – and they all appear alive in the depictions. Living prisoners would have been valuable, thus making them a viable part of the Meroitic economic system.

In point of fact, slaves were traded to Egypt for linen under the terms of the *baqt* agreement in the medieval period (*c.* AD 500–1500). Furthermore, during his travels to Shendi between 17 April and 17 May 1822, John Lewis Burckhardt commented on what he considered to be the most important element of their economy: the slave trade. He estimated that each year the market sold around 5,000 slaves, of which about half were carried off by Souakin merchants and an additional 1,500 taken by Egyptian merchants.[7] Burckhardt also mentioned that there were at least 40,000 slaves in Egypt at the time of his visit, but that it was a reflection of the most moderate count.[8]

Salt mining also became an important economic practice. The need for salt, or more specifically natron, in temple rituals may have had an impact on the location chosen for the temples.[9] A Nubian temple at Sonijat had salty deposits in the area next to the southern end. These deposits have been utilized by Bedouins and the people of Abkur as salt is added to the bread and *kisra*. Locals have claimed that the salt has been quarried around the temple for longer than anyone can recall.[10]

Unlike hunters and gatherers, salt has to be added to the food of people in sedentary societies since their limited diet does not provide the required daily amount. Salt is also needed for the preservation of perishable foods and the treatment of cow hides. In Ptolemaic Egypt the production and sale of salt was monopolized by the royal house. Strabo was the only writer to comment on salt sources during the Kushite period, and only to the extent of stating they quarried the mineral.[11] Therefore, salt was important not only in the temple rituals but as a tangible commodity, which could explain why the temple at Sonijat was built in that particular location.

Salt was also a prominent commodity in the West African trans-Saharan trade route since it could be traded for both low- and high-quality items. Kushite rulers may have utilized salt in the same manner as the Ja'alin chiefs described by Burckhardt in 1822 in his book *Travels in Nubia*. High concentrations of salt were located in the area of Taragma at Buweida. He mentioned that the salt-filled earth was collected by the Arabs and heaped along the side of the road. The soil would then be boiled in large earthenware vessels to separate the salt, which would be boiled a second time in smaller vessels.[12] Once quarried and treated, the salt would be formed into cakes, which had the appearance of rock salt, packed in a basket and traded around Sudan. The salt trade became a primary commodity of the Shendi Reach peoples and was under the sole control of the ruler, or *mek*, who had about twenty vessels with earth boiling at the time of Burckhardt's visit.[13] Sennar merchants would purchase Buweida salt in large quantities and transport it to the Abyssinian border to trade for gold or slaves.

Nubian society

Nubian society evolved over the course of its history. In the earliest periods, settlements were composed of temporary dwellings made from perishable materials, which enabled the people to move around based on the seasonal migration of herds and available vegetation. As groups became more sedentary, settlements arose of permanent houses made of mud-brick with stone details and foundations. Houses developed organically and had a combination of curved and straight walls depending on space allowances. They were generally composed of public and private areas and could house several generations under a single roof. Enclosure walls were built around the settlements for protection. Eventually, differences in social status could be seen based on the size of a dwelling as well as the lavishness and quantity of grave goods placed alongside the deceased.

Cattle were unsurprisingly important, and were used for many purposes. Typical attire included leather garments such as loincloths for the men and pleated skirts for the women. Linen tunics, kilts and skirts could be worn by men and women, often atop the leather loincloths. In the Napatan period (c. 800–300 BC) men and women started wearing a new garment known as a 'Kushite cloak', which was a fringed cloak worn over a kilt, skirt or dress, and could be tied either at one or both shoulders. They also wore sandals or walked barefoot. From the earliest periods, the Nubians liked to adorn themselves with jewellery. They made bracelets, necklaces, rings and earrings out of semi-precious stones, faience and metals.

The Nubians were famed archers throughout their history, yet little is known about the organization of the army. The ruler would have been the leader of the military, as seen in many ancient and modern cultures. It is uncertain whether being a member of the army was a profession or if the postings were temporary. However, the king and queen probably had a permanent security force. When not serving in the military, Nubian men would have been found working the fields, tending the animals and participating in construction projects. The women, meanwhile, would have maintained the home, participated in craft production, such as pottery and weaving, and raised the children.

The economy relied on a combination of agriculture and animal husbandry along with commerce. The Nubians frequently traded with their neighbours to the north and east and a barter system was in place for much of their history. Money as we think about it was not widely used until the Christian period (AD 614–1400) and, even then, not every site accepted the coins as viable currency.

Entanglement of cultures and ideas

It is undeniable that Nubia and Egypt had contact with each other from their earliest periods. However, the manner in which this connection has been studied, historically, has tended to focus on Egypt's power and influence over the 'lesser' culture of Nubia. This type of analysis does not allow for the native Nubian culture to be recognized as an entity unto itself. More recent studies have begun focusing on how the Nubians integrated Egyptian culture into their own while still maintaining the elements that defined them as Nubian. This is known as 'cultural entanglement', which allows for a more inductive and inclusive approach that does not favour one cultural tradition over another.[14]

Remains from the site of Tombos in the Third Cataract region demonstrate the practice of cultural entanglement during the New Kingdom Egyptian colonization of Nubia and the transition into the Napatan period, through the analysis of cultural and biological links that emerged and developed during these periods. While buildings dating to the New Kingdom colonization and Napatan period in Nubia do have Egyptian elements, the Nubian style of architecture can clearly be seen in the funerary culture. Burial practices are an integral element of cultural expression and can demonstrate how a group accepts and interprets death and the afterlife.[15]

At Tombos, graves were covered with Nubian-style grave superstructures, but the burials themselves were an amalgamation of Egyptian and Nubian cultural influences: sporadic evidence of the use of coffins and mummification, amulets of Egyptian deities (particularly Bes, Ptah-Pataikos, Isis and Hathor), placing the deceased on a Nubian-style funerary bed, and sometimes laying the deceased in a flexed position.[16] Evidence from excavations at Amara West and Sanam also demonstrate the use of both Egyptian and Nubian burial customs and a combination of grave goods.[17]

It is also important to consider the Egyptianization model, which is the notion that culture was only transferred from the north to the south (that is, from Egypt to Nubia). This is not an accurate assessment of the contact between the two cultures. The

Egyptianization model assumes that all levels of society wanted to aspire to adopt Egyptian symbols and ideology, yet the model does not account for degrees of acculturation within cultural groups (such as social class, gender and age).[18] Many groups within Nubia would have had little or nothing of value to gain from assimilating into the Egyptian way of life. Furthermore, the Egyptianization model does not allow for Nubian influences on Egyptian culture. Some of the most notable examples of this are the ram imagery for the gods Amun and Ra, the tightly curled and cropped hairstyle, and the leather kilts worn by soldiers, farmers and workmen. During their interaction, culture and ideology were transferred between the two countries and the relations were two-sided. Ultimately, cultural exchange was not simple, linear or one-directional, but equally influenced by both the Egyptians and Nubians.

Travellers to Nubia

As early as the eighteenth century European travellers journeyed southwards to explore the land of Nubia. One of the earliest was Frederik Ludwig Norden (1708–1742), a Danish naval captain, who visited the Temple of Derr, built by Ramesses II, in Lower Nubia. He became the first European to journey south into Nubia, documenting landscapes and peoples seen along his voyage. The account of his journey was published posthumously as *Voyage d'Egypte et de Nubie* (1755).

With the 1798 Napoleonic invasion of Egypt, more Europeans became fascinated by Egypt, and Nubia by extension, leading to regular journeys into these foreign lands during the nineteenth century. Muhammad Ali Pasha commissioned the service of Frédéric Cailliaud (1787–1869), a traveller and mineralogist, and Louis Maurice Adolphe Linant de Bellefonds (1799–1883), a geographer, explorer and engineer, to investigate the remaining emerald and gold resources in Sudan. Cailliaud travelled as far south as Meroe and published his *Voyage à Méroé, au fleuve Blanc au delà de Fazoql, dans le midi du royaume de Sennar, à Syouah et dans cinq autres oasis fait dans les années 1819, 1820, 1821 et 1822*, in which he documented the pyramid fields at Meroe. Linant de Bellefonds was the first European to visit Musawwarat es-Sufra and Naqa and documented the monuments he found along his journey.

George Waddington (1793–1869) was an English traveller who visited Nubia around the time of the Ottoman conquest by Muhammad Ali Pasha in the 1820s. He published his Nubian journey, *Journal of a Visit to Some Parts of Ethiopia*, in 1822. He thought he had discovered Meroe when he visited Jebel Barkal, which was later disproven when Cailliaud and Linant de Bellefonds made their explorations in Nubia.

Karl Richard Lepsius (1810–1884), a German Egyptologist, led a Prussian expedition to Egypt and Nubia between 1842 and 1845. He travelled throughout both countries documenting the monuments he saw, eventually publishing his drawings and notes in a twelve-volume series titled *Denkmäler aus Ägypten und Äthiopien* (1849–56). His records remain some of the most important to the field since many of the monuments he documented were destroyed by flooding to enable the construction of Nile dams and are no longer available for study.

The twentieth century brought about the scientific study of Nubia and intensive surveys of sites throughout the country. Francis Llewellyn Griffith's (1862–1934) interest in Egyptology was sparked when he read the works of Giovanni Belzoni (1778–1823). He began his career excavating at sites in the Egyptian Delta and spent his later life excavating at the Nubian site of Kawa. He was a renowned philologist and accomplished a preliminary decipherment of the Meroitic script. The English Egyptologist Cecil Mallaby Firth (1878–1931) worked with George Reisner on the *Archæological Survey of Nubia* (1907–10) and completed preliminary excavations at the Temple of Sanam near Napata in 1912. John Garstang (1876–1956), an English archaeologist, extensively excavated the royal city of Meroe from 1909 to 1914.

The American Egyptologist George Andrew Reisner (1867–1942) worked throughout Egypt and Nubia. His accomplishments include excavations at the Nubian capitals and cemeteries of Kerma, Napata (Jebel Barkal) and Meroe, as well as forts in the Second Cataract region. He is considered one of the founding fathers of Nubian studies.

Since this time, dozens of archaeological expeditions from around the world have taken place in North Sudan and continue to this day, revealing countless discoveries and re-imaging of the histories and cultures of Nubia.

TWO
FROM NOMADS TO LEADERS

W hen trying to cover tens of thousands of years of a culture's history, it can be a challenge deciding where to start. Nubia had a long and rich history long before its colonization by Egypt in the New Kingdom (*c.* 1550–1070 BC). In an attempt to demonstrate the length of this history, we will begin in the Palaeolithic period, which is characterized by fluctuations between wet and dry periods in Africa versus the ice ages and warm periods in present-day Europe and North America. During the Palaeolithic, Mesolithic and Neolithic periods, stone tools were used for hunting, gathering and fishing. From there we will explore how environmental changes led to new subsistence strategies, social hierarchies, and impressive pottery and artefact production. The rise of the kingdom of Kerma, when the Nubians became notable participants in ancient Africa's development, will conclude our journey.

Palaeolithic period

Palaeolithic culture sites have been found throughout Lower and Upper Nubia and even south of Khartoum along the Blue and White Niles. This period can be divided into three phases: Early Palaeolithic (*c.* 1,000,000–100,000 BP), Middle Palaeolithic (*c.* 100,000–34,000 BP) and Late Palaeolithic (*c.* 34,000–10,000 BP). Date ranges from this period are designated by BP or 'Before Present', where 'present' is defined as 1 January 1950. These time designations are frequently used in archaeological and geological contexts. Following the Palaeolithic period, dates ranges switch to BC, and eventually AD, which will be used for all subsequent periods.

Palaeolithic faunal remains indicate that the environment was much wetter than it is today and probably consisted of open wooded grasslands. Palaeolithic peoples practised hunting and gathering as their subsistence strategies and were mostly nomadic. Buildings are rarely found from this period because they were made of perishable materials such as wood and animal skins. However, we do have physical remains from these groups in the form of stone tools for hunting game, fishing and fowling (hunting and trapping wild birds).

The earliest Palaeolithic Nubian cemetery is at the site of Jebel Sahaba near the Second Cataract. The deceased were buried in oval pit graves usually consisting of multiple interments. The discovery of stone flakes embedded in the bones led to the original assumption that these people were killed violently during a territorial dispute; the skeletal remains, however, indicate that the population was healthy and was not wiped out during a single event.[1]

Mesolithic period

The Mesolithic period (c. 8000–5000 BC) is divided geographically into the Khartoum Mesolithic in Upper Nubia from the Third Cataract south and the Khartoum Variant in Lower Nubia. Khartoum Mesolithic sites are located near the Nile or seasonal water sources, whereas Khartoum Variant sites are located near the Second Cataract and Batn el-Hajar regions.

These sites consisted of widespread dwelling areas with artefacts such as grindstones, suggesting semi-sedentary occupation of the areas. The inhabitants subsisted primarily on hunting and fishing, along with grass and seed gathering.[2] Burials were typically associated with dwellings. The deceased was placed on their right side in a contracted, foetal position. There were no grave goods associated with the burials.

The Mesolithic period was also known for its abundance of microlithic stone tool technology, as well as an established ceramic industry. Pottery produced during this time was of high quality with thin walls and was well fired.[3] The pots were decorated with incised wavy lines and impressed zigzag lines that covered their entire surface. Ostrich eggshell and stone disc-shaped beads were also produced during this period.

Nubian Neolithic

The Neolithic period (*c.* 4900–3000 BC) can be divided into two phases: Early or Khartoum Neolithic (*c.* 4900–3800 BC) and Late Neolithic (*c.* 3800–3000 BC). The desertification characteristic of Sudan today was not the environment present during the Neolithic period. At that time the region was warm and humid, allowing habitation sites to be located away from the Nile in areas that have long since been abandoned due to lack of water resources.[4]

Sites are identified by dense scatters of potsherds, lithics, grindstones and bone. Archaeological remains similar to the ones found near Khartoum were discovered as far north as the Second Cataract. This suggests a northward migration since the artefact assemblages indigenous to Lower Nubia differed from those of the Khartoum region. Seasonal camps were used in conjunction with year-round habitation sites. The temporary camps were used for herding and fishing during the dry season. Dwellings at these temporary camps were constructed of grass/reed or reed/grass mat huts and some settlements possibly had communal hearths.[5]

Subsistence strategies still relied upon hunting and fishing, yet during the Neolithic period we start to see the transition from fully hunter-gatherer groups to the beginnings of animal husbandry.[6] With the shift to pastoralism, the diet began to include animal products such as milk and possibly blood in addition to meat. The cultivation of crops is difficult to identify in the archaeological record, so it is uncertain whether the cereal remains were from wild or domesticated plants. The increased presence of sheep and goats may suggest that the environment was becoming drier, causing the Neolithic Nubians to adapt their subsistence strategies.[7]

The pottery industry was similar to its predecessors, producing wares decorated with dotted and incised zigzag lines.[8] Calciform

Skeletal remains from Jebel Sahaba.

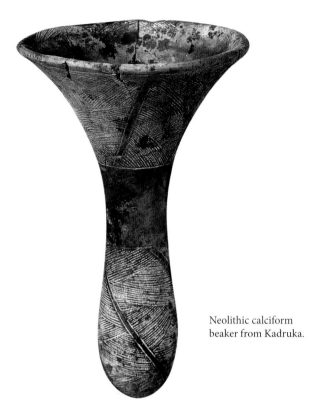

Neolithic calciform
beaker from Kadruka.

beakers were manufactured during the late Neolithic with rocker
stamps used to create the surface designs. The decorative elements
were filled with white gypsum to highlight the patterns.[9] Items of
personal adornment such as beads, bracelets and pendants continued to be produced.[10]

Neolithic cemeteries consisted of circular pit graves with the
bodies placed in a contracted, foetal position. At this time the
custom of placing grave goods around the bodies began and an
individual's status could be determined based on the quantity and
quality of the items found within their grave.[11] At some sites stelae
are used to mark the grave; at others there is evidence for human
and animal sacrifice. Cattle skulls (bucrania) were also placed in
the tombs as grave offerings, emphasizing the importance of cattle
in Neolithic culture.[12]

A-Group

The A-Group (*c.* 3800–2900 BC) was a culture centred primarily in Lower Nubia between the First and Second Cataracts. This period is divided into three phases that were contemporaneous with the end of the Predynastic and Early Dynastic periods of Upper Egypt: Early A-Group (Naqada I and II, *c.* 4000–3200 BC), Classic A-Group (Naqada III, *c.* 3200–3000 BC) and Terminal A-Group (Naqada III to Dynasties 1 and 2, *c.* 3200–2686 BC). With the similarities between Nubian and Egyptian pottery from these time periods, Reisner assumed that the Egyptians had migrated southwards and established a new settlement. Today, however, the A-Group is recognized as a culture that is undoubtedly Nubian.

Although connections to the earlier Neolithic groups in Lower Nubia can be identified in the A-Group, distinct developments that occurred during this period show that progress was being introduced in the country: the domestication of cereal grains, the rise of domestic architecture, the development of a specific pottery type of red-and-black vessels, and the implementation of burial practices. Because the domestic architecture was generally constructed from perishable materials, most of the information we have about the members of the A-Group come from their cemeteries and the goods they placed alongside their deceased.

The diagnostic pottery from this period consists of various vessels that have a polished, red exterior with a black interior and rim. This style of pottery, which became increasingly popular during the Naqada period, can be found along the Nile Valley. The vessels discovered in Nubia, however, were locally produced, highlighting the transmission of ideas between the two countries. Through interactions between the early groups of Egyptians and Nubians, black-topped pottery became a popular style and continued to be used by the Nubians for another 1,500 years, long after the Egyptians abandoned it.

Domestic architecture does not survive well in the archaeological record, but from the scant remains it appears that the dwellings were temporary nomadic huts, which would allow the group to migrate based on their seasonal needs. Many of these dwellings were constructed of grass and reeds held together by mud. Remains of hearths and storage pits are sometimes found at the camps. An interesting discovery was found at the site of Afyah, located in the Korosko bend. Here, there are remains of stonework buildings and at least one house (*c.* 200 square metres/ 2,150 sq. ft) with up to six rooms, along with storage pits and traces of mortar and plastered walls.[13] Various objects were found associated with this house including stone tools, bone and copper awls, and Egyptian and Nubian style pottery. The complexity of this house may be an indication of the shift to a more sedentary lifestyle for elite members of the society.

While the domestication of crops is patchy in the archaeological record, there is evidence that wheat, barley, lentils and peas were grown. These crops are characteristic of the onset of sedentary societies in northeastern Africa and southwestern Asia. Along with the beginnings of farming, the Nubians also began raising their own animals such as goats, sheep and cattle. Even though the members of the A-Group were growing their own crops and raising their own animals, these practices were not sufficient for the entirety of the diet, which had to be supplemented with continued hunting and gathering, as well as fishing. The Nubians also traded for speciality goods and products such as wine and oils.

Cemeteries and burials dating to the A-Group show that the culture was becoming more interested in the afterlife, increasing social stratification was becoming apparent, and trade with other countries, particularly Egypt, had begun. Graves at this time included pits that were nearly circular and oval pits with a chamber cut on one side. The graves generally did not have superstructures but were instead covered with large stone slabs. The bodies were placed within the graves in a contracted, foetal position with the head usually facing to the west. The burials in the First Cataract region show the bodies were wrapped in mats or linen, whereas in the Second Cataract region the bodies were wrapped in animal skins.[14]

Grave goods placed in the tomb included Egyptian and Nubian objects such as pottery, stone vessels, palettes, copper and bone tools, incised ostrich eggshells, incense burners, clay figurines,

Conical eggshell-ware bowl dating to the A-Group.

items made from lapis lazuli, as well as seals and seal impressions. Along with the objects placed around the body, the deceased would have been adorned with pendants, bracelets, amulets and ivory combs. Animals, such as dogs, sheep, goats, gazelles and cattle, were also sacrificed and buried in the grave with the deceased or in the cemetery.[15] Burials of humans together with animals was also practised at the Egyptian site of Hierakonpolis, so it is possible that the Nubians were emulating their northern neighbours.

There is evidence for the beginnings of social complexity and hierarchy in the A-Group cemeteries. Here, burials of different ages, genders and social standings were shown through the quantity and quality of luxury grave goods placed in the tomb along with the body. Additionally, the size of the grave and its location

Animals depicted on a mace from Seyala.

in relation to the largest and most luxurious graves may also indicate the status of an individual. Particularly impressive burials have been found at the sites of Qustul (Cemetery L) and Seyala (Cemetery 137), located between the First and Second Cataracts. At Qustul, of the 25 tombs that were excavated, there were eight particularly large tombs that have been identified as belonging to a ruling class.[16] The graves were rectangular in shape with a chamber cut into the side. Many of the graves contained multiple individuals, of varying genders and ages, buried together. Remains of wooden beds offer some of the earliest evidence for this Nubian burial tradition. Along with the burial beds, finely manufactured pottery was also found in the graves as well as imported objects from Egypt and the Near East. Cemetery 137 at Seyala also showed evidence of early social complexity. Grave goods found in tomb 1 were particularly lavish and included two Egyptian maces with their handles covered in gold. The smaller of the two maces has elaborate decoration on the handle, comprising five registers of animals including an elephant stepping on two serpents. This object was probably a gift to the Nubian leader from an Egyptian ruler.

By the end of the A-Group, local and regional chiefdoms were already developing, which the Egyptians may have viewed as a threat to their southern border. An Egyptian early dynastic graffito from Jebel Sheikh Suleiman, located near the Second Cataract, shows the victory of an Egyptian king over Nubians.[17] The right side of the scene shows four defeated Nubians underneath a boat with a fifth one attached to the prow by a rope tied around his neck. Another Nubian is shown on the left side of the scene with his hands tied behind his back. The centre of the graffito shows two

Graffito from Jebel Sheikh Suleiman.

Ivory or bone bead from the tomb of Djer dating to the Early Dynastic Period.

circles with an 'x' inside each one. This is the Egyptian symbol for a place name specified by the images on top of each. The dating of this graffito has been debated because no clear king's name can be identified in the *serekh*, an image of the palace facade with a Horus falcon sitting on top. However, parallels with beads as well as ivory and lapis lazuli objects from the tomb of the Dynasty 1 king Djer from Abydos show similar serekhs of the falcon on top of a building facade with dots in between.[18] The graffito was removed prior to the flooding of the area by Lake Nasser and can be found in the Khartoum National Museum. The A-Group people were driven away from Lower Nubia during the Egyptian late Dynasty 1 or early Dynasty 2 and did not return to the area for another six hundred years.[19]

C-Group

The C-Group (*c.* 24/2300–1600 BC) was also located in Lower Nubia in the First and Second Cataract regions. This period is divided into three phases that were contemporaneous with the

Upper Nubian Kerma cultures and the Egyptian Old Kingdom through the Second Intermediate Period: Early C-Group (c. 2685–2008 BC, Kerma Ancien/Egyptian Dynasties 6–8), Middle C-Group (c. 2008–1685 BC, Kerma Moyen/Egyptian Dynasties 11–early 13) and Late C-Group (c. 1685–1550 BC, Kerma Classique/Egyptian Dynasties late 13–17). When Reisner identified the C-Group, he did not equate it with an Egyptian-influenced culture but rather recognized it as completely Nubian.

The C-Group culture probably did not originate in Lower Nubia but instead consisted of groups from Upper Nubia that migrated north and possibly shared a common origin with the Kerma culture. It was during this time that Egyptian Old Kingdom incursions into Nubia occurred, perhaps to monitor the influx of peoples into the region. A military campaign was documented on a fragment of a Dynasty 5 (c. 2494–2345 BC) king list known as the Palermo Stone.[20] The inscription records the defeat of a group of Nubians who were 'hacked up' by the Egyptian army. After the battle, the Egyptians returned with 7,000 prisoners and 200,000 head of cattle. Assuming these numbers are not an exaggeration, this would have been a devastating blow to the Nubians.

As with the A-Group, much of the information we have about the C-Group comes from their cemeteries. C-Group burials were similar to those of their predecessors and consisted of oval or rectangular burial chambers with the bodies placed on their right sides in the fully or partly contracted foetal position, and their heads were generally placed to the east. The bodies were adorned with beads, bracelets, armlets and hair rings that can also be found in Kerma Ancien (c. 2500–2050 BC) burials. Grave goods were arranged around the body and consisted of locally manufactured and imported objects. Although the presence of metal objects in graves was rare, some graves contained bronze mirrors and daggers.

Unlike the A-Group graves, tombs dated to the C-Group had superstructures in the shape of tumulus mounds atop the burial. This style of grave was also common in the Kerma Ancien period and beyond. In the later C-Group phase, rectangular mudbrick extensions were constructed along the eastern sides of some of the

C-Group drinking cup from Faras.

tombs for visitors to leave offerings. This arrangement is similar to Egyptian tomb superstructures.

The pottery from this period consists of a continuation of the black-topped red wares found in the A-Group contexts as well as a local Nubian type of shiny black vessels incised with geometric designs. The decorative elements would be filled with chalk or talc after the vessel was fired, creating white designs on a black background that is characteristic of the C-Group. Unlike contemporaneous Egyptian pottery, which was wheel-made, Nubian pottery continued to be handmade.

Although the early phases of the C-Group peoples still lived in temporary, seasonal camps, from their earliest beginnings C-Group communities were socially stratified, and it appears that within a century of migrating into Lower Nubia, the rulers of the chiefdoms were living in permanent residences.[21] At the site of Aniba archaeologists discovered the remains of a village that consisted of earlier tent dwellings, each with a centre pole and a fireplace. In a later level, mud and stone semi-subterranean houses were discovered. These mid-level structures were either single-room dwellings or multi-room complexes.[22] The latest occupational level at Aniba showed the construction of small, rectangular mudbrick rooms, which are similar to Egyptian-style houses. One of the best examples of a later C-Group settlement is at the site of Wadi es-Sebua, where more than one hundred stonework houses were constructed. These consisted of both circular and rectilinear buildings surrounded by a defensive wall. The arrangement of this settlement is comparable to the mid-level structures found at Aniba.[23]

The Nubians still practised pastoralism, raising sheep, goats and, especially, cattle, which were then highly valued and central to the cultural ideals. Clay models and bucrania of cattle have been found in the cemeteries, and depictions of cattle are also present on C-Group stelae, pottery and rock art. The bucrania were typically associated with the largest graves of higher-status members. The degree to which the C-Group peoples participated in agricultural practices is unclear, but the shift to a more sedentary lifestyle towards the end of the period does indicate that they were farming to a certain degree.

Contact between Nubia and Egypt during this period has been documented in the tomb autobiographies of Egyptian officials, as will be discussed later. During these expeditions, the Egyptians encountered many well-established Nubian groups, indicating that the country was quite prosperous during the C-Group period. A Dynasty 6 (c. 2345–2181 BC) Egyptian official at Aswan had the title 'Keeper of the Door to the South' or 'Overseer of the foreign countries', suggesting that the Nubians were establishing themselves as a notable neighbour and as a potential threat to the prosperity and dominance of the Egyptians.[24]

When the Old Kingdom began to decline during Dynasty 6, it is possible that the Egyptians could no longer lord it over the Nubians in the same way they had during their heyday of Dynasties 4 and 5. In Dynasty 6 the Egyptians also abandoned their settlement at Buhen, in the Second Cataract region, as well as the diorite quarries that had become so popular during the earlier Old Kingdom. The relatively peaceful relations between Nubia and Egypt during the First Intermediate Period (c. 2160–2055 BC) may have allowed for the local Lower Nubian rulers to consolidate power and turn their attention north. In order to control their neighbours to the south, the Egyptian Middle Kingdom kings of Dynasty 12 constructed a series of fortresses in the Second Cataract region. At this time, any power that the C-Group leaders had amassed was stifled because the Egyptians were now able to control the flow of goods and peoples into and out of Nubia.[25]

During the Second Intermediate Period (c. 1650–1550 BC) Egyptian control over Nubia waned, allowing for the northern advance of the Kerma peoples. Evidence of the C-Group culture eventually disappeared during the New Kingdom (c. 1550–1070 BC) colonization of Nubia.

Pre-Kerma period

The Pre-Kerma period (c. 3000–2500 BC), contemporaneous with the Classic Terminal phases of the A-Group in Lower Nubia, was centred in Upper Nubia in the Third Cataract region and extended as far north as the Second Cataract. Although most of the remains discovered date from the latter phases of the A-Group, evidence for occupation as far back as 4700 BC has also been found, indicating a much longer use of the site. This period was first identified by Charles Bonnet, who has been excavating at the site of Kerma since the 1970s.

One of the excavated settlements is located under the Eastern Cemetery at Kerma. When the Nile began drying up at the end of the Neolithic period (c. 4900–3000 BC), the residents moved west to the site of Kerma, the first ancient capital of Nubia. By this period the shift to settled, sedentary societies had occurred and the Pre-Kerma inhabitants practised agriculture along with animal husbandry.[26] The location of the Pre-Kerma settlement was later reused during the Kerma Moyen phase as a cemetery.

Postholes indicate that several types of buildings were constructed at the site, including approximately fifty round huts, two rectangular buildings, enclosure walls and animal pens.[27] The rounded huts range in size from 1 to 7 metres (3–23 ft) in diameter, suggesting that the structures served various functions. The bases of the huts were constructed by weaving branches between the posts and covering the structures with mud. The roofs would have been conical and made from reeds or grasses. This type of dwelling can be found in East Africa today.[28] The smaller posthole rings probably indicate areas used as animal pens, whereas the largest ones might have served as communal meeting places or as the residences of higher-status individuals.[29] One of the rectangular structures was oriented east–west and was rebuilt three times throughout its lifespan.[30] The second building was located at the edge of the settlement and oriented north–south. These buildings probably served as spaces for special functions.

Along with the postholes, 285 storage pits have been discovered to date, although up to five hundred storage pits are estimated.[31] The pits were mostly empty, but they probably contained food storage jars. Pre-Kerma material has also been found at Sai Island, near the Third Cataract, where storage pits contained mud seals for jars as well as pottery,suggesting a well-established and maintained settlement.[32] The storage pits at Kerma appear to have been emptied prior to the abandonment of the site, since they were intentionally backfilled.[33]

Pottery remains, such as pots, bowls and jars, have served as the primary basis for the identification of the Pre-Kerma occupation. The vessels typically have a well-polished surface and were sometimes decorated with a chevron pattern. Pottery from this time could also have a red or black colouration. There are similarities between the Pre-Kerma and Kerma ceramics, which indicates a level of continuity between the settlements. Evidence for relations with Egypt during this period is not widely available.

Kerma period

The first major capital of Nubia, at the site of Kerma, is located about 4 kilometres (2½ mi.) west of the Pre-Kerma settlement. This period, known as the Kerma period, is divided into three phases: Kerma Ancien (Ancient) (c. 2500–2050 BC), Kerma Moyen (Middle) (c. 2050–1750 BC) and Kerma Classique (Classic) (c. 1750–1450 BC). At its height the kingdom of Kerma probably ranged from Kurgus, between the Fourth and Fifth Cataracts, to Aswan in the north.

Western Deffufa at Kerma.

In Egypt, indications of a yet unknown culture were found through the discovery of Kerma Classique pottery in Second Intermediate Period and New Kingdom tombs. Early excavations were conducted by George Reisner from 1913 to 1916, during which time he discovered a multitude of Egyptian material including statues, stelae and vessels, which led him to identify the site as an Egyptian colony.[34] When excavations by Bonnet began in the 1970s, Reisner's theory that Kerma was an Egyptian outpost was re-examined and scholars realized that the site was the home of a powerful Nubian culture.

At the heart of the ancient capital stood a monumental mud-brick construction known as the Western Deffufa, which served as the city's main temple. Early travellers commented on the def-fufas, which were named after an ancient Nubian term for any unfired mudbrick fortification.[35] The temple was approached and entered from the side rather than the front, which differed from the temples that would be built following the New Kingdom colonization of Nubia. The building was enhanced over the course of its history and, by the Kerma Classique, dominated the landscape.

The settlement developed around the Western Deffufa. Early dwellings of tents and huts were similar to those of the Pre-Kerma settlement. Unfired mud-brick, however, eventually became the dominant building material. In the later phase of the settlement's development, secondary chapels, workshops and storerooms were constructed around the temple. A bronze-maker's workshop was discovered near the main temple, indicating that some of the bronze objects were locally manufactured.[36] Residences dedicated to the priests or rulers were built near the temple. At the eastern side of the site, large bakeries provided bread and beer for temple offerings. By the end of the Kerma period, the Western Deffufa had become the predominant building in the town's landscape.

Around 2000 BC a fortification wall with bastions and entrance gates surrounded the town. This wall was expanded over time as the population at Kerma increased. As the town grew, defence systems improved; walls were faced with fired bricks and buildings were enhanced with stone foundations.[37]

To the south of the temple, a circular structure was discovered that is typical of the architecture found at Kerma in both royal and non-royal contexts. This building was a large hut measuring at least 10 metres (33 ft) high and constructed of wooden posts and a rounded mudbrick wall that would have supported a conical roof.[38] Within the building is a brick wall outlining a large 12-square-metre (129 sq. ft) room with two adjoining rooms and passages. A building of this type and size dating to the Kerma period has no parallel in Egypt or central Africa; similar buildings of later date, however, can be found in Darfur and southern Sudan.[39]

During the Kerma Classique a new palatial building was constructed and would have replaced the earlier large, round hut. The structure was arranged in three distinct sections: the royal apartments in the east, the throne room and administrative buildings in the centre, and the storage areas in the west.[40] There was a corridor in the northern portion of the palace that led into an inner courtyard. A second courtyard, rounded in shape, was located behind the inner courtyard, which added to the available meeting space for the building.

The throne room was constructed within the inner courtyard and was approached via a vestibule flanked by small rooms that may have served as archives. Inside the vestibule was a well that contained more than 5,000 clay seals, suggesting a high degree of movement of goods. The three large pillars within the throne room suggest a roof height of approximately 5 metres (16 ft), which is comparable to the large funerary chapels in the necropolis at Kerma.[41] The throne room was divided into two sections: the first was at the side and accessed by two separate entrances, and the second was where the king would have been seated on his throne, atop a dais accessed by a ramp or staircase.

In the western portion of the building were the food storage areas and possibly pens for domesticated animals. There were two silos, measuring approximately 7 metres (23 ft) in diameter, with the capacity to store up to 30 tonnes of grain.[42] Storage areas of this type were utilized in association with the palace by the last kings of Kerma.

The eastern cemetery fields of Kerma were centred around another large mudbrick temple called the Eastern Deffufa. Although only the mud-bricks used to construct the temple are visible today, the Eastern Deffufa would have been decorated with glazed faience tiles in antiquity. Fragments of a large-scale lion faience inlay were found near the facade of the temple. This was one of two such inlays that probably flanked the entrance to the temple. Wall paintings of African animals, boating and fishing scenes, and fighting cattle also once adorned the walls. The Eastern Deffufa was connected to the final royal burial (KIII) at the cemetery.

This cemetery consisted of approximately 20,000 graves which can be dated to all three phases of the Kerma period. Burials consisted of circular or oval graves with stone and earth superstructures. The deceased was placed on their right side in a contracted, foetal position between leather covers. Some clothing remains have been unearthed, including a loincloth or a long skirt

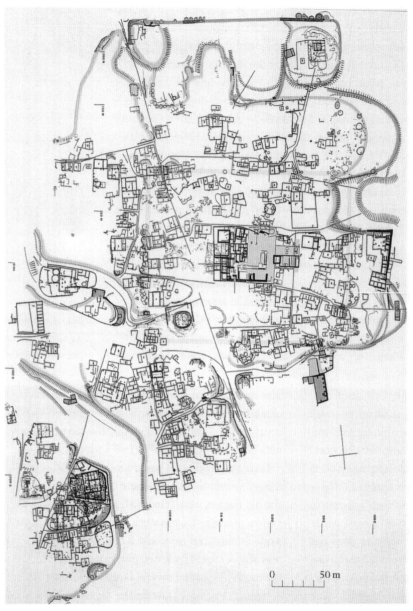

0   50 m

Topographic map of the settlement at Kerma.

Faience lions from Eastern Deffufa.

Modern reconstruction of a footboard from a Kerma funerary bed.

tied across the stomach with the upper body covered in a leather or linen garment.[43] These garments were decorated with faience or shell beads sewn into the fabric. Some female burials show the women's heads adorned with leather hair nets.[44] The deceased also typically wore decorated sandals. The people of Kerma did not mummify their deceased and they placed the body on a bed rather than in a coffin. By the end of the Kerma Ancien, this practice had become common.[45] These burial beds were decorated with bronze or ivory inlays of animals and mythical creatures, including winged giraffes and a Nubian version of the Egyptian goddess Taweret. Grave goods of wooden or bone rings, earrings, bead necklaces, pottery and ostrich feather fans were also placed within the tombs.

Nubians were famed archers who served in the Nubian and Egyptian militaries. Tombs of these soldiers have been found that date to as early as the Kerma Ancien. The archers were buried with a bow, quiver of arrows and their daggers. Some of the skeletons still have their archers' rings around their thumbs.[46]

During the Kerma Moyen phase, sheep and goat burials alongside the deceased became more prevalent and chapels were also added to the western side of the tombs for offerings. The deceased continued to be placed on top of a funerary bed, around which were arranged various objects such as jewellery, pottery and ostrich feather fans. Social stratification of the tombs became more apparent at this time and large tombs, measuring between 30 and 40 metres (98–131 ft) in diameter, probably belonged to Kerma Moyen princes or kings.

The kingdom of Kerma established complex political and religious systems during the Kerma Classique. The kings were buried under huge tumuli, measuring as large as 100 metres (328 ft) in diameter, constructed of mudbrick walls underneath a giant earth superstructure. Vaulted burial chambers, located at the centre of the tumuli, contained the king's body. The pathways to the burial chambers were lined with the skeletons of human sacrifices who were to serve the kings in the afterlife.[47] Lavish grave goods including beds decorated with ivory or bronze inlays, statues and various vessels were discovered inside the tombs.

The cemetery showed evidence of social stratification through the size of the tombs, luxuriousness of the grave goods, and the presence of animal and human sacrifices associated with the tombs of the rulers. The inclusion of human sacrifices in royal and elite burials during the Kerma Classique was a product of the increasing power of the Kerma state. This practice would have been a result of changes in social dynamics by which, in various ways, non-elite members of society would become bound to members of the elite or royal classes and repay their debts through sacrifice at the time of the elite's or royal's death.[48] It is unclear how the sacrificial people were killed, but the skeletal remains suggest that the deaths may have been via poisoning or suffocation.[49]

Evidence for funerary feasts can be found in the cemetery and date to its earliest use. In the northern part of the cemetery, vessels were found placed upside down to allow for sharing food between the living and the dead.[50] Along with these vessels, remains of beer filter straws were found, suggesting the use of these communal straws during the commemorative feasts to create strong social bonds.[51] The presence of cattle bucrania buried on the south side of some tombs was also possibly connected to funerary feasts. The number of bucrania present varies and one elaborate Kerma Moyen tomb, probably for a member of the royal family, had 4,000 bucrania associated with it.[52]

Kerma period pottery is similar to that of the C-Group, which is probably a result of continued contact between or a common origin of these two groups. These handmade vessels were typically polished black-topped red wares, or black, reddish-brown or buff wares.[53] They were decorated with the traditional geometric patterns including diamonds, chevrons and zigzags. One of the most impressive firing techniques originated from the Kerma Classique phase. During this time a grey metallic band was added between the black mouth and red body of the cups and beakers. This was achieved by placing the vessel upside down on an organic substance that oxidized during the firing process.[54] These vessels have become an iconic representation of the fine skill and craftsmanship of the Kerman potters.

Throughout the Kerma period we can also see the development of regional settlements that are tied to the religious and political capital of Kerma. Settlement sites such as Gism el-Arba, H25 and Es-Selim R4 were designed to provide agricultural, pastoral and manufactured products for use in the capital as need increased. They also served as sites of collection and distribution to accommodate the expanded trade with neighbouring cultures. Evidence of occupation at these sites spans throughout the Kerma period and beyond. Architectural remains from Gism el-Arba demonstrate similarities with those at the capital, highlighting a shift from circular huts to rectangular mudbrick structures built on top of stone and/or wood foundations.[55] The high presence of goat, sheep and cattle remains at sites such as Gism el-Arba may be due to the increased demand for animals and their products by the capital.[56] Renewed and continued excavations of these sites will shed additional light on the relationships between the capital at Kerma and these regional centres.

Kerma tomb showing bucrania.

Kerma Classique beaker.

During the Kerma Moyen/Classique phases, contemporary
with the Egyptian Second Intermediate Period (*c.* 1650–1550 BC),
Egyptian power declined. As a result the ruler of Kerma formed
an alliance with the Hyksos ruler in the Delta and together they
ruled northern and southern Egypt respectively, while the native
Egyptian rulers continued to control the Theban region. This
collaboration almost led to the downfall of the Egyptians, but in
approximately 1500 BC the Egyptians succeeded in defeating the
Hyksos and Kerma rulers and reunified Egypt. They would pro-
ceed to conquer Nubia and rule over it for approximately the next
five hundred years.

THREE

NUBIA AND EGYPT

The relationship between Egypt and Nubia spanned over 3,000 years and the two regions can best be described as 'frenemies'. The ancient Egyptians regarded themselves as the ultimate country in all regards. They viewed their surrounding countries as lesser and therefore only valuable when considering how they could serve Egypt. Nubia was no exception: the gold-rich hills of Nubia supplied most of the gold used by the Egyptians to secure their place in the ancient world.

Although Nubia and Egypt undoubtedly had contact in the earliest phases of their histories, it was during the Egyptian Old Kingdom (*c.* 2686–2125 BC) that relations between the two countries began to be formally documented by the Egyptians. It is through their artistic and textual accounts that we can gain knowledge of their interactions; however, it is important to note that these records are solely from the Egyptian perspective. It is through the archaeological evidence that we get the other side of the story and see that the Egyptians were not always the ones dominating the conversation.

Nubia during the Old Kingdom

A person's desire to explore the world around them is a common human curiosity, equally apparent among the ancients as it is for us today. Documentation of contact between Egypt and Nubia can be found from Egypt's earliest records and became more prevalent during the Old Kingdom. These texts highlight the Egyptians' desire for the coveted products – gold, ivory, ebony, precious stones, exotic animals and animal skins, and incense – of their neighbour to the south.

Although early contact between Nubia and Egypt appears to be a mixture of peaceful and contentious encounters, Egyptian officials of Dynasty 6 (c. 2345–2181 BC) led diplomatic expeditions to Nubia and documented their travels on their tomb walls. These texts detail their experiences and the items they brought back to Egypt.

The first known traveller to Nubia was an official named Weni, who served under kings Teti, Pepy I and Merenra.[1] During the reign of Merenra, Weni was sent to Nubia to quarry granite and to construct barges and ships out of acacia wood from Wawat that had been cut down by the rulers of Irtjet, Wawat, Yam and Medja.[2] After completing his tasks within a year, he journeyed back to Egypt.

One of the most famous travellers to Nubia was Harkhuf, a governor of Upper Egypt under kings Merenra and Pepy II. He led at least four diplomatic journeys to the south and his autobiography provides some of the best insights into Old Kingdom relations with Nubia.[3] During his first trip he travelled with his father and was expected to 'open up the way' to Yam. Since he successfully completed this expedition over the course of seven months, his next journey to Nubia was a solo mission. Harkhuf's second trip involved exploring the regions of Irtjet, Mekher, Tereres and Iertjetj over the course of eight months. According to his autobiography, no one had travelled through these areas before his expedition. On his third journey to Nubia, Harkhuf was again sent to Yam and found that the ruler had moved to the land of the Tjemehu in the west, so Harkhuf went to find him. During this trip, he realized that the lands of Irtjet, Satju and Wawat had been unified, indicating that some sort of internal battle had taken place. His fourth recorded expedition occurred during the reign of Merenra's successor, Pepy II. Along with the typical resources brought back from the land of Nubia, Harkhuf returned with an additional present for the boy king: a dancing pygmy. This present was lauded by Pepy II, 'all because of the joy in the heart of my majesty at the sight of this pygmy'.[4]

Despite the Egyptians' love for the resources of Nubia, they viewed dying there as undesirable and considered it an urgent and pressing matter to bring back the body for burial in Egypt. An example of this is the account of the Old Kingdom official Sabni, the last known traveller to Nubia, who journeyed south to retrieve his dead father's body.[5] In preparation for his trip, Sabni loaded donkeys with Egyptian products that would serve as gifts for the Nubians holding his deceased father. To protect his father's body, Sabni transported it in a lidded wooden coffin that he had brought from Egypt. Upon his return, Sabni had his father's body properly embalmed and buried according to Egyptian customs. Because he had successfully journeyed to Nubia and retrieved his deceased father, along with the goods that his father had acquired in the foreign land, Sabni was given a reward from Pepy II.

An Egyptian Old Kingdom settlement at Buhen in Lower Nubia suggests the establishment of trade networks between Egypt and Upper Nubia. This town would have enabled the Egyptians to exploit the extensive Nubian natural resources located throughout the area and have them brought to a central location to be tallied and prepared for transport back to Egypt. Jar sealings and ostraca with the names of Dynasty 5 (c. 2494–2345 BC) kings indicate this administrative centre was in use during the height of the Egyptian Old Kingdom.

Second cataract forts in Nubia

Following the decentralization of the Egyptian government during the First Intermediate Period, the Egyptians sought to regain control over Nubian resources as well as the Nubians themselves, who had proved to be a threat to Egyptian control. The Old Kingdom town at Buhen laid the groundwork for the Middle Kingdom (c. 2055–1650 BC) rulers who built a series of forts in the Second Cataract region of Lower Nubia. Amenemhat I (c. 1985–1956 BC) began constructing mudbrick forts at Ikkur, Kuban, Aniba and Buhen. These sites positioned the Egyptians at critical areas of Nubia: Ikkur and Kuban were at the entrance to the Wadi Allaqi and Wadi Gabgaba, where gold and copper were mined, and Aniba

Military ration token from the Middle Kingdom fort at Uronarti. Markings indicate quantities of grain or products to distribute to the soldiers.

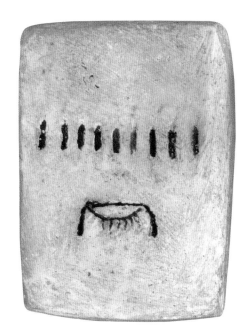

Stone weight used for weighing gold, representing 116 g (4 oz) of gold.

was at the centre of the C-Group territory.[6] From Amenemhat I to Senwosret III (*c.* 1870–1831 BC), fifteen forts were constructed and renovated along the Nile.

The forts were pinnacles of bureaucratic administration with up to five hundred soldiers controlling the C-Group peoples, monitoring mining expeditions, smelting and preparing gold to be shipped back to Egypt, and conducting trade relations with the growing town of Kerma. Although not solely militaristic in nature, the Egyptians did recognize the need for fortifying the sites, and so built defensive mudbrick enclosure walls around the forts. Along the walls were bastions to monitor the landscape and openings for the archers to loose their arrows if the fort was ever under attack. Later forts were also constructed atop rocky outcrops, allowing the Nile to provide additional protection.

The forts were self-contained settlements with barracks for the soldiers, commanders' quarters, temples, storerooms and silos for storing grain. Architectural and ceramic remains indicate that the forts' occupants comprised both Egyptians and Nubians. Activities at the forts can be reconstructed through seal impressions, military ration tokens, royal boundary stelae and letters known as the 'Semna Dispatches'.

Ration tokens found in the fort at Uronarti look like conical and round loaves of bread, a typical form of ancient Egyptian payment. These tokens have inscriptions that state how much grain the token was worth.[7] Stone weights were also discovered at Uronarti that were used for weighing gold that had been mined and was being processed for shipment back to Egypt.[8] The hieroglyphic sign for gold (Egyptian 'nebu') and lines indicating the weight can be seen on the stones.

Senwosret III had boundary stelae placed at the southern border where the fortresses of Semna and Kumma established Egyptian control over the area and restricted northward movement by the Nubians. One of the inscriptions highlights the king's low opinion of the Nubians by stating, 'They are not men of worth. They are wretched, broken hearted.'[9] Many of the forts were also named to reflect Egyptian dominance over the Nubians, such as 'Destroying the Nubians' (Askut) and 'Warding off the Bows' (Kumma).

The 'Semna Dispatches' are a series of letters written on papyri, now fragmentary, sent from Egypt to the forts as well as between the forts. These texts document the movement of goods and peoples as well as the administration of the region. The communications also mention the treatment of the traders, which included payment for the goods as well as rations of bread and beer.[10] The dispatches could have travelled at a relatively quick pace, going from Elephantine to Semna West, a distance of approximately 425 kilometres (264 mi.), in 21 days.[11] This would have included time for the courier (or couriers) to stop at forts along the journey south. Along with the 'Semna Dispatches', letters were written by a head official in Egypt and sent to the commanders at the forts. Two such letters describe inspections of peoples and the activities of the forts' commanders performed by an Egyptian official travelling through Nubia.[12]

Based on textual evidence, some of the forts remained in service towards the end of the Middle Kingdom. A letter mentioning the rotation of soldiers at the forts dates to early Dynasty 13 (c. 1773–1650 BC), a statue with the cartouche of King Sobekhotep IV on Argo Island, and statues at Mirgissa and Semna with inscriptions that possibly refer to King Wagef suggest an Egyptian presence in Nubia during the later Middle Kingdom.[13]

Kerma and Egypt

Although the first mention of Kerma in Egyptian documents did not occur until Dynasty 12 of the Middle Kingdom, there is possible evidence for diplomacy between the two countries during Dynasty 6. This is based on fragments of commemorative stone vases inscribed with the name of Pepy I which may have served as gift exchanges between the rulers.[14]

During the Kerma period (c. 2500–1450 BC) there was continual contact between Nubia and Egypt. Nubians raided the southern portions of Egypt and brought back spoils of their expeditions to the capital. One of the most famous statues pillaged from Egypt is that of the Lady Sennuwy who, along with her husband, had a tomb at Assiut in Egypt. The statue, however, was discovered in

Statue of the Lady Sennuwy dating to the Middle Kingdom.

Decorative rosettes from Eastern Deffufa.

tomb KIII, which was intended for one of the rulers of Kerma who lived about 350 years after her death.[15] Such statues were one of the reasons George Reisner believed Kerma to be an Egyptian out-post in Nubia. Egyptian objects looted from Egypt during military campaigns would have been prominently displayed at Kerma to emphasize the Kerman king's authority and power.

An attack on Egypt by the kingdom of Kerma and its allied forces was documented in an inscription from the tomb of the gov-ernor Sobeknakht at el-Kab. The text states that the Kushites (that is, the Kerma army), along with allies from Wawat, Khenthennefer in Upper Nubia, Punt and the Medjay, made their way northwards and possibly campaigned as far north as the Hyksos capital in the Delta.[16] The Egyptians at el-Kab rallied and travelled south to fight the Nubians. This inscription indicates that Kerman control extended further north and encompassed more territory than has previously been thought.[17]

Although relations between Kerma and Egypt could be contentious, there is also evidence for the admixture of cultural ideas. Objects found in the eastern cemetery at Kerma highlight this blending of motifs, where the object itself was made in Nubia by local artisans using local materials, while incorporating Egyptian stylistic elements.[18] Beautiful carved ivory pieces that decorated the funerary beds at Kerma highlighted local flora and fauna as well as this blending of materials and iconography. Images include representations of the Egyptian goddess Taweret, shown wearing a kilt and carrying a dagger, as well as the Egyptian-style winged sun disc and vulture.[19]

Along with the Egyptian-inspired imagery, the Kerman rulers also repurposed Egyptian objects for other uses. Decorative rosettes from the ceiling in the Eastern Deffufa were made using fragments of Egyptian faience objects that were shaped into the rosette design.[20] Traces of the original black decoration on these reused pieces can still be seen.

The alliance between the king of Kerma and the Hyksos ruler in the Delta was documented on the second stela of Kamose found at Karnak.[21] The inscription notes that the future king intercepted a messenger from the Hyksos capital at Avaris (modern Tell el-Dab'a) who was running south to Kerma. In the letter, the Hyksos ruler was encouraging the king of Kerma to march north with his army so the two could crush the Egyptian rulers at Thebes and divide Egypt among themselves. Kamose recognized his dangerous position, caught between these two powers, and wrote, 'To what effect do I perceive it, my might, while a ruler is in Avaris and another in Kush, I sitting joined with an Asiatic and a Nubian, each man having his (own) portion of this Egypt, sharing the land with me?'[22] Ultimately Kamose and his army were able to defeat the Hyksos ruler and prevent an assault from the south. He then set about a reunification of Egypt that would lead to the establishment of the New Kingdom, during which time the Egyptians would colonize and control Nubia.

Nubia during the New Kingdom

After he ascended to the throne and completed his campaigns in Asia, Ahmose, the founder of the New Kingdom (*c.* 1550–1070 BC), focused on reclaiming Lower Nubia for Egypt. He reoccupied the fortress at Buhen and established a temple there. Ahmose or his son, Amenhotep I, managed to conquer Nubia south of the Second Cataract. During the reign of Thutmose I, Egyptian expeditions continued even further south to the Fifth Cataract region. He established a fort at the Third Cataract site of Tombos, which allowed control of river and land traffic, and secured the gold-mining regions. Thutmose I's successors continued to expand their claim over Nubia as far south as the Fourth Cataract region.

Ahmose and his successors also recognized the need to monitor Egypt's southern border and created a new office to govern the region, known as the viceroy of Nubia.[23] The position began as a militaristic one where the viceroy was sent to Nubia as the commandant of Buhen. During the reign of Thutmose IV the officials were granted additional titles, such as King's Son of Kush, although it is highly unlikely that an actual prince of Egypt held the position. The viceroys would have reported directly to the king, which was a privilege reserved for few high-ranking officials and priests.

These officials decorated their tomb walls with tribute scenes. One of the most famous collection of scenes is in the tomb of the viceroy of Nubia, Amenhotep, called Huy, who served during the reign of Tutankhamun. The scenes show rows of Nubians bringing tribute to the official, who receives them on behalf of the king.[24] Items being presented include gold in rings, bags of gold, carnelian or red jasper plates, green mineral plates, white ivory tusks, ebony, a model chariot of gold, shields, furniture and a golden shrine.

Three Nubian princes, identified as the 'chieftains of Wawat', approach Huy. Two of them kneel in adoration and the third, the prince of Mi'am (Aniba), Hekanefer, prostrates himself before the viceroy. They all wear leopard skins with finely embroidered

Nubians bringing tribute to Amenhotep, called Huy (detail from his tomb, Theban Tomb 40).

sashes, feathers in their hair and large earrings. Tribute bearers are shown behind the entourage carrying more gold, animal skins and giraffe tails.

Behind the tribute bearers, a princess is shown riding in a chariot drawn by cattle. The use of cattle to pull a chariot is unexpected since Egyptian royal chariots were traditionally pulled by horses. The use of cattle instead of horses may have been a way for the artist to insult the Nubian princess, since she was not granted the same quality of animal in the depiction as Egyptian royalty. Another possibility is that cattle were so prized by the Nubians that they would have been the animal of choice to drive a royal chariot. The princess is shaded by an ostrich feather parasol, again showing the importance of ostrich feathers to the Nubians.

In the second register the princes of Upper Nubia and their retainers are shown. Their attire is similar to that of the princes of Lower Nubia and they carry tribute such as giraffe tails and feline skins. They even offer a live giraffe, possibly for the king's menagerie.

One of the last viceroys of Nubia was Panehsy, who held the office during the reign of Ramesses XI (*c.* 1099–1069 BC). He is known from two documents dating from years twelve and seventeen of the king's reign. The first papyrus is a list of grain that was distributed to the tomb workmen at Thebes, where Panehsy was acting under his title 'Overseer of the Granaries'. The second papyrus is a letter from the king to his viceroy to ensure that Panehsy would cooperate with the king's butler, Yenes, to bring back Nubian products to the palace.

Panehsy's career was filled with scandal, including his participation in the suppression of the High Priest of Amun, Amenhotep, who was threatening the king's power, and leading a revolt with the assistance of his Nubian forces. During the war of Panehsy, numerous letters were written by a scribe of the necropolis named Dhutmose (Tjaroy), who travelled from Thebes to Elephantine and eventually to Nubia. He documented the assembly of the army and the acquisition of resources such as weaponry, food and bandages. The general Piankh also wrote letters outlining his plan of action to suppress the revolt. Following the rebellion, he was vilified by the new High Priest of Amun, Herihor. Little is known about Panehsy once he returned to Nubia, but presumably he was buried at Aniba, which served as his base during the rebellion. Egyptian military authority was not restored in Nubia following the rebellion and the Egyptians lost control over valuable natural resources and vital trade routes.

During the reigns of Amenhotep III and Tutankhamun, the Third Cataract site of Soleb served as the primary administrative centre in Upper Nubia. Later, during the Ramesside period, Amara West possibly replaced Soleb. Egyptian control of Nubia eventually extended to the Fourth Cataract region and Thutmose III began construction projects at Napata (modern Jebel Barkal). Although Egyptian-style monuments were built at Napata and inscriptions written in Egyptian hieroglyphs have been found, the administration of the area between the Third and Fourth Cataract was possibly in the hands of local Nubian elites.[25]

New Kingdom temple towns

Following the New Kingdom reconquest of Nubia, the Egyptians built temple towns in the Third Cataract region that enabled them to exercise their authority over the Nubians. These towns were typically comprised of an Egyptian-style temple, industrial sectors and residential areas, all surrounded by an enclosure wall, fortifying the town. The areas where the towns were constructed have evidence of occupation ranging from periods prior to the New Kingdom and as late as the Islamic period. A look at a few examples of these administrative centres can tell us about the impact of the Egyptian New Kingdom colonization.

At the beginning of Dynasty 18, Sai Island became the first Egyptian outpost in Lower Nubia and remained as such until Dynasty 20.[26] At the end of the New Kingdom the fortified town was abandoned by the Egyptians, yet there is evidence of occupation into the Islamic period. The pharaonic town at Sai Island, located approximately 180 kilometres (112 mi.) south of Wadi Halfa, was established on the northeastern bank of the island. It is surrounded by an enclosure wall that was reinforced with square brick towers. The town was arranged on a north–south axis with entrance gates at the western and southern enclosure walls.[27] Although the Egyptians were aware of Sai Island during the Middle Kingdom, the site continued to be under the control of the king of Kerma until the New Kingdom. This site was considered to be a threat to Egyptian control and expansion to the south. Sai Island is the only known large settlement site of the Kerma culture, other than Kerma itself, and has even been referred to as a 'sub-capital of the Kushites'.[28]

At the beginning of Dynasty 18, Ahmose or Amenhotep I (c. 1550–1504 BC) established the town, thereby ending Kerma control in this area. The attribution of Ahmose as the founder of the fortified site is based on a broken statue of the ruler found at Sai Island. Also found at the site was a similar statue of his son Amenhotep I which shows him seated wearing the jubilee *heb-sed* cloak, a short robe ending at the mid-thigh and wrapping around the torso, leaving the hands exposed. The similarities between the statues could have been an homage to Ahmose by Amenhotep I. The site was used through-out the early New Kingdom and the construction of the temple dates to the reign of Thutmose III, based on foundation deposits and a text dedicated by the viceroy of Nubia, Nehy.

The earliest remains indicate that the town was modelled or remodelled after traditional pharaonic towns.[29] In its southern portion, a large-scale domestic building, possibly for government officials, was identified along with houses containing storage areas and silos.[30] The industrial sectors were located in the northern portion of the town where storage areas, ovens and grinding imple-ments have been found.[31] This area would have been responsible for preparing bread, possibly for temple offerings. The pottery found in the northern area indicates that activities beyond household tasks and living were being performed. Vessels for storage, food pro-duction and consumption, feasting and religious activities, such as incense burning, as well as imported vessels have been identified.

The site of Sesebi is located on the west bank across from the modern town of Delgo. This temple town, along with Kawa, was presumably established during the reign of Akhenaten (*c*. 1352–1336 BC), the Egyptian king who attempted to establish monotheism. This attribution is based on foundation deposits, dating to his early reign, discovered under the corners of the enclosure wall and main temple.[32] The northern temple at Sesebi also shares similarities with the design of religious structures found at Amarna dating to the latter portion of Akhenaten's reign, indicating the site was used throughout his rule. There is also evidence that the site was still in use until the early Ramesside period, when it was abandoned.

Sesebi may have been devoted to mineral extraction activ-ities. Evidence of gold mining has been found to the north and south of Sesebi and may have taken place at this site as well since excavations have revealed grinding stones for gold processing. These types of grinding stones were introduced during the reign of Thutmose I, signifying that the area was being exploited for gold during the New Kingdom colonization.[33]

Sesebi has two temples within the main enclosure wall. Both of these temples were constructed during the reign of Akhenaten:

the first during his early reign prior to his name change from Amenhotep IV to Akhenaten and the second during the later Amarna period. Decorated plaster and stone fragments show a mixture of pre-Amarna and Amarna-period imagery. The Amarna-period carvings were recarved during Dynasty 19 with images of the king Seti I.[34]

As at Sai Island, there were residential and industrial quarters at Sesebi. A concentration of bread mould fragments near the main temple could indicate the location of the temple bakeries.[35] Houses at Sesebi were built of mud-brick with stone architectural details. The houses are aligned in long rows with an adjoining house on the east and west, with a wide street separating them from the enclosure wall. One of the houses (F.6.13) has the remains of a staircase that probably led to the roof. The houses have evidence of a kitchen with ovens and storage areas. The larger houses (F.6.13, F.6.22) are similar in style to the Amarna elite houses, suggesting that these houses at Sesebi were built by Egyptians or designed by Egyptian architects.

Pottery found within the fortified town included Egyptian, Nubian and imported wares. The Egyptian types have been dated to late Dynasty 18 and include fragments of amphorae, one-handled mugs and pilgrim flasks.[36] Interestingly, blue painted pottery, a type common during the Amarna period, has not been found. Nubian pottery includes potsherds of Kerma beakers and handmade vessels with basketry impressions on the exterior. Imported amphorae from Canaan and the western oases were also discovered.

The Dynasty 19 king Seti I (c. 1294–1279 BC) chose Amara West as the site for his new town, which was called the House of Menmaatra (Seti I).[37] Amara West is located on a small island just north of Sai Island. As with the other temple towns, Amara West was occupied during the New Kingdom and may have remained in use until as late as Dynasty 25, when Nubia ruled Egypt.

The original site was surrounded by a mudbrick enclosure wall constructed of bricks that were stamped with the king's name. This enclosure wall had bastions along it, corner towers and a walkway along the top so guards could patrol the area.[38] The Temple of

Statue of Amenhotep I, from Sai Island, dating to the
New Kingdom.

Amun-Ra occupied about a quarter of the area within the walled town. This temple may be dated to the reign of Ramesses II, the son of Seti I, based on the decorative programme and two commemorative stelae. One of the stelae recorded Ramesses's marriage to a Hittite princess; the other recorded a dream in which the pharaoh received a blessing from the god Ptah.[39]

The layout of the temple was modelled directly upon New Kingdom Egyptian examples, placing it in a clear context with New Kingdom construction. The walls of the peristyle court were adorned with hieroglyphic inscriptions dating to Year 6 of Ramesses IX (c. 1126–1108 BC), one of the last Ramesside rulers, probably commemorating the end of the decoration in the temple. This is the last known New Kingdom royal inscription found in Upper Nubia.[40]

A large residential building, which has been identified as the Deputy's Residence (E13.2), had inscribed door jambs and lintels listing several deputies (idnw), including Sebaukhau, who served under Seti I, and Paser, who served under Ramesses III (c. 1184–1153 BC).[41] These deputies would have reported directly to the viceroy of Nubia. A second large house (E12.10), located outside of the walled town, along with six other 'villas' at the site show similarities with New Kingdom elite houses, underscoring the presence of Egyptian architectural styles at Amara West. The closest Nubian comparative building to Villa E12.10 is a large house recorded at Aniba.[42] During Dynasty 20 Aniba became the seat of the deputy of Lower Nubia, thus justifying the construction of a large-scale residence at the site.

Clay seal impressions have been found underneath the floor of E12.10. Some of the seals bore the throne name (praenomen) of Thutmose III, while others had various decorative motifs. These seal impressions are indicative of the presence of a functioning Egyptian bureaucracy at Amara West.[43] A pottery fragment with a hieratic copy of an excerpt of the *Teaching of Amenemhat to His Son Senwosret* was also found underneath the floor of E12.10. This potsherd was similar to one, discovered at Amara West in 1938–9, that also had a copy of the *Teaching* written on it. These sherds are the first copies of the classic Middle Egyptian literary text discovered outside of Egypt.[44] The presence of the *Teaching of Amenemhat* at Amara West is the first example proving that formal Egyptian scribal training was taking place outside of Egypt. It remains unclear, however, whether those who were actually using the *Teaching* were impacted by the anti-Nubian elements within the text.[45]

During the New Kingdom colonization, building projects continued at an area known as Dokki Gel, or 'red hill', located about 1 kilometre north of the town of Kerma.[46] Although this area was considerably expanded during the reign of Thutmose I, there is evidence that the site was in use during the Kerma Classique period.[47] The establishment of a New Kingdom addition to Dokki Gel by Thutmose effectively marked the end of Kerma rule in Nubia.

With an enclosure wall surrounding the town, Dokki Gel is similar to the other New Kingdom temple towns established during the colonization. Within the enclosure wall, a temple to the god Amun, two palaces, storerooms, bakeries and a well were discovered.[48] The buildings were modified or rebuilt throughout Dynasty 18 and the site was in use through the Meroitic period. One big difference between the traditional New Kingdom temple towns and Dokki Gel is that the architecture at this site shows a true blending of indigenous Nubian and imported Egyptian construction styles.

Along with the construction of temple towns, the Egyptians also introduced new burial practices to the Nubians. At this time pyramids were constructed for the elite Nubians as well as Egyptians living in Nubia. The pyramids were built using local Nubian sandstone and had chapels attached to them. Additionally, the Nubians shifted from being buried in a contracted position on a bed to an extended position, sometimes in a coffin.[49] Decorations within the tombs also reflected the adoption of Egyptian imagery. The incorporation of Egyptian burial styles made the tombs of the Nubian elite almost indistinguishable from those of the Egyptians.

Nubians in Egypt

We have seen that contact between Nubia and Egypt has been consistent throughout their histories, yet we have only looked at the Egyptian presence in Nubia and not the other way around. Nubians travelled into and throughout Egypt from the Predynastic period until the Assyrian invasion of Egypt in 664 BC. They lived and worked among the Egyptians and intermarried. Nubians who chose to stay adopted and adapted Egyptian cultural practices and became complete members of Egyptian society.

At Hierakonpolis, a site located about 113 kilometres (70 mi.) north of Egypt's southern border of Aswan, Nubian C-Group cemeteries have been found. The tombs show an integration of Egyptian styles along with the Nubian elements.[50] Unlike C-Group tombs in Nubia, the ones at Hierakonpolis used mud-bricks instead of stone and constructed vaulted burial chambers. Nubian-style pottery was found in the tombs, indicating they were using a combination of

Middle Kingdom Egyptian model of Nubian soldiers from the tomb of Mesheti at Asyut.

Stela of Nenu.

their native techniques with local materials. Egyptian-style wares were discovered along with the Nubian-style vessels in the tombs. The Nubians adopted wooden coffins for burial yet still dressed the deceased in leather garments. One well-preserved, coloured leather skirt found in the tomb of a female was made from a series of leather panels stitched together using a drawstring to secure the garment. Leather loincloths and beaded belts were found in several male burials. Decorated sandals were also discovered. Hairstyles were also reminiscent of Nubian traditions: skin impressions left by the garment show that one woman wore a leather hair-net and several people had braided hair.[51]

Beginning in Dynasty 6, Nubians had not only achieved notoriety as archers but become mercenaries in the Egyptian army. They continued to serve in the Egyptian military through the

First Intermediate Period and into the reunified Middle Kingdom. Images of Nubian soldiers can be found on the walls in the tomb of Ankhtifi at Mo'alla. Along with these images, an inscription there lists his titles, including 'Commander of the Nubian mercenaries'.[52] Therefore, the Nubian soldiers were probably under the command of an Egyptian official rather than a fellow Nubian soldier.

There is evidence of the soldiers marrying Egyptian women and being buried according to Egyptian traditions. These inter-marriages were documented on stelae found at and near the site of Gebelein. These stelae often label the male as 'nehesy', which was the designation for someone who came from Nubia. The deceased's dog is typically shown as well, suggesting that dogs held an important place among the Nubian soldiers. One such stela shows the Nubian soldier Nenu and his Egyptian wife Sekhathor along with their children and dogs, as well as a servant. He and their children are shown with darker skin and wearing Nubian-style attire, while his wife wears a traditional Egyptian sheath dress and is shown with the yellowish skin typical of an Egyptian woman.

During the Middle Kingdom models were made showing scenes of daily life, including scenes with models of Egyptian and Nubian soldiers. The Nubian soldiers are carrying bows in their left hand and arrows in their right. They are shown with darker skin, a white band in their hair, and wearing short kilts with a red tie or overlay, whereas the Egyptian soldiers wear traditional white kilts. The red colour of the kilt sashes connects these wooden figures with the representations of Nenu and his children as well as the Nubian princes in the tomb of Huy. Bowls decorated with Nubian hunters were also discovered at Aswan. An example shows a dark-skinned Nubian man in traditional attire and again holding a bow in his left hand and arrows in his right. He is accompanied by his dogs, one of which is also participating in the hunt.

The movement of Egyptians into Nubia and Nubians into Egypt emphasizes the deep connections these cultures had with one another. One of the most impactful contributions was the introduction of the Egyptian writing system into Nubia. Although the Nubians were using a foreign language, the use of hieroglyphic writing finally allows us to read about Nubian history from the Nubians themselves. The Egyptian abandonment of Nubia (*c.* 1070 BC) was due to another period of decentralization of the country and duelling power bases at Thebes and in the Delta. The end of colonization, however, did not mark the end of Nubian history, but instead it allowed the Nubians to reclaim their country and embark upon their own age of imperialism.

FOUR
WHEN NUBIA RULED
THE (ANCIENT)
WORLD

Following the Egyptian colonization of Nubia, the country fell into a so-called 'dark age' marked by a lack of written texts and archaeological remains dating to the time between the end of the colonization and the beginning of the Egyptian Dynasty 25 (c. 760–656 BC) and the subsequent Napatan period (c. 800–300 BC). The legacy of the New Kingdom colonization could be seen through Egyptian hieroglyphs, Egyptian-inspired architecture and decorative arts, and the integration of Egyptian kingship and religion with the indigenous Nubian ideologies.

Although we lack information from this time, some sites have managed to shed light on what was happening following the withdrawal of Egypt. At Hillat el-Arab, located in the Fourth Cataract region, nineteen tombs dating from the late New Kingdom to the Egyptian Dynasty 25 have been discovered.[1] Although the superstructures are no longer preserved, the subterranean chambers are able to tell us about the peoples and funerary customs during this interim period.

The tombs are decorated with blended imagery, such as boats, and grave goods, including imported amphorae and storage jars, copper-alloy bowls, as well as scarabs and small amulets. There are no coffins or funerary figures (*shawabtys*) in the tombs, yet traces of a funerary bed were found in tomb 1. Remains of horse burials in some of the tombs shows that the Napatan practice of kings burying their beloved horses near their tombs was already established among the elite.

Tombs dating to the time between the colonization and the Napatan rulers were surprisingly lavish compared to what would be expected from an interim period. Trade with Egypt and southwest Asia continued and items such as pilgrim flasks and imported amphorae have been found in the tombs.

Lower Nubia was largely depopulated following the New Kingdom, possibly as a result of climate change and the aridification of the region. Small cemeteries have been found but not many are outside the Second Cataract region, where cemeteries and small temples were constructed or reconstructed.

The administration of Nubia reverted back to local chiefdoms, which ultimately paved the way for the rise of a new group of rulers. During the first millennium BC a new capital was founded at the site of Napata (Jebel Barkal) near the Fourth Cataract.

Egypt's Dynasty 25

The founding of the dynasty in the eighth century BC has been attributed to an obscure ruler named Alara. He is not known from the archaeological record but rather through references to him in texts. His role as the first Napatan king was revered even in later centuries, when kings would declare their legitimacy by linking themselves to Alara and his family line.

Kashta (c. 760–747 BC) succeeded Alara and set his sights northwards towards Egypt. Although he may not have journeyed beyond Aswan, his northward march marked the first attempt at Nubian expansion into Egypt since the Kerma period. Kashta may even have been crowned at Thebes, yet the exact details of how he accomplished this remains unclear.[2]

Around 747 BC Piankhy (Piye) (c. 747–716 BC) succeeded Kashta and began his first campaign into Egypt, probably in his fourth regnal year. This campaign may have resulted in the expansion of his rule to Thebes, after which he returned to Nubia and enlarged the Amun Temple at Napata.

The Libyan ruler at Sais, Tefnakht, began marching southwards c. 728 BC. At this point Tefnakht had secured rulership over the western Delta from the Memphite region to the Mediterranean, yet he desired control over more of Egypt. After Tefnakht defeated Nimlot, the ruler of Hermopolis in Middle Egypt, Piye took notice of his opponent's southward advance and sent his troops to fight against the rebellion. Although they were successful, defeating rebels at Oxyrhynchus, killing the son of the Chief of the Ma, Tefnakht, and fighting Hutbenu, Piye was not satisfied, causing him to sail north on the ninth day of the first month of the inundation.

Piye systematically attacked the rebellious cities, thus causing the local rulers, Peftjauawybast in Herakleopolis, Nimlot in Hermopolis, Iuput II in Leontopolis and Osorkon IV in Bubastis, to surrender one by one. Following this campaign, Piye returned again to Napata, where he erected his Great Triumphal Stela.[3] This details his conquests and the lunette (top) of the stela shows the defeated rebels in supplication to him. Piye is also depicted as a true Egyptian who was superior to his Libyan opponent and ultimately the rightful ruler of Egypt.

Piye was succeeded by his brother Shabaqo (c. 716–702 BC). The Nubian succession did not always pass from father to son; if the son of the king was considered too young to rule, then the king's brother, or sometimes a cousin, would succeed him instead.[4] Shabaqo also campaigned into Egypt, eventually conquering Memphis and celebrating his coronation at the ancient capital, thus marking the official beginning of Dynasty 25 in Egypt. Due to the Egyptian king Bakenranef's attempt to maintain control over Sais in the Delta, Shabaqo relocated his capital from Napata to Memphis in order to squash his opposition. Diplomatic relations continued with the Assyrian Empire during the reign of Sargon II after Shabaqo sent Iamani, who led a revolt against Sargon II and attempted to flee to Egypt, back to the Assyrian capital.

Great Triumphal Stela of Piye.

Primary building activities during his reign occurred at Thebes, where he restored existing temples and re-established Nubian rule. One of the most important texts describing an Egyptian creation story, known as the Memphite Theology, dates to the reign of Shabaqo. The text was inscribed on a block of basalt after Shabaqo discovered a worm-eaten papyrus with the story written on it. He wrote his epithets on top and the creation story on the right-hand side. Before the stone was identified it had been used for grinding grain, so some of the story is missing. This version of creation is centred around the god Ptah, the primary deity of Memphis, who created the world through his mind and words.

Shabaqo died at Memphis and his body was transported back to Nubia so he could be buried at the royal cemetery at el-Kurru. He was succeeded by his son Shabitqo (c. 702–690 BC), who almost immediately began fighting the Assyrians in western Asia for control of Egypt, calling upon his family for support, including his cousin and successor Taharqo. Sennacherib's army was forced to retreat, and Taharqo and his forces returned to Egypt.[5] Shabitqo's reign was short but appears to have been relatively peaceful. He was buried at el-Kurru alongside his predecessors.

Taharqo (690–664 BC), following in Shabaqo's footsteps, was crowned at Napata and Memphis to affirm his control over both countries. In his sixth regnal year he erected a stela at Kawa on which he was named as the heir apparent, declaring that he was preferred over all brothers and children of Shabitqo.[6] In that year the Nile inundation and rainfall in Nubia were particularly high, and Taharqo claimed that these events were proof of Amun's favour:

His Majesty had been praying for an inundation from his father Amen-Rê, lord of the Thrones of the Two-lands, in order to prevent dearth happening in his time. Well, then, everything that comes forth upon His Majesty's lips, his father Amûn makes it happen at once. When the time for the rising of the Inundation came, it continued rising greatly each day . . . Every man of Bow-land (Nubia) was inundated with an abundance of everything, Black(-land) (Egypt) was in beautiful festival, and they thanked god for His Majesty.[7]

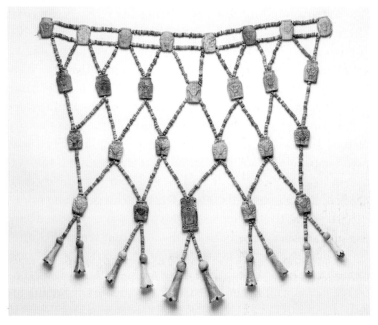

Bead net for a horse from el-Kurru dating to the reign of Shabaqo.

Along with the abundant fertility resulting from the high water levels, insects, rodents, snakes and damaging winds were all banished from the region.[8]

During this time the Nubians conducted trade with the Assyrian Empire and imported Lebanese cedar, Asiatic copper and chariot horses called *kusayya*, or 'Kushite'.[9] In Year 17 of Taharqo's reign, however, the Assyrian king Esarhaddon moved his forces west and succeeded in reclaiming the region of Palestine. Two years later Esarhaddon made another attempt to conquer Egypt and eventually succeeded in capturing Memphis, sending extensive booty, including Taharqo's heir, back to Assyria.[10] At some point Taharqo probably reclaimed Lower Egypt for Nubia but he was eventually defeated by Esarhaddon's successor, Assurbanipal, who captured Egypt as far south as Aswan and installed Assyrian vassals to control the country in his absence. Taharqo returned to Nubia and remained at Napata until his death.

Overall, Taharqo's reign was one of prosperity and active building projects in Nubia and Egypt, particularly at administrative

Pyramids at Nuri.

centres such as Napata and Thebes. His construction programme may have been indicative of his desire to consolidate power between Nubia and Egypt and create a centralized government unifying the two countries into one vast territory.[11]

Tanwetamani (c. 664–656 BC) succeeded his cousin and began a systematic attempt to reconquer Egypt. He received support from the Nubian authorities stationed at Thebes and managed to recapture Memphis and send loot back to Napata. He continued north and defeated and killed the ruler Necho at Sais. Upon hearing about Tanwetamani's exploits in Egypt, Assurbanipal launched another invasion in 664/663 BC, even burning Thebes and raiding the temple coffers.[12] Tanwetamani continued to rule at Napata until his death, although Nubia would never again regain control of Egypt.

The ruling family established a royal cemetery at el-Kurru, about 12 kilometres (7½ mi.) downstream of Jebel Barkal. It is uncertain whether the earlier tumulus tombs belong to direct royal ancestors of this dynastic line or if they pre-dated the founding of the Napatan familial line. Regardless, there was a shift in tomb construction from the traditional tumulus graves to pyramids.

The pyramids were built using small blocks of Nubian sandstone with chapels attached on the eastern side. The burial itself was located underneath the pyramid and accessed by a flight of stairs. Along with the pyramids, 24 horse burials, associated with Shabaqo, Shabitqo, Piye and Tanwetamani, have been found. The horses were outfitted with royal trappings (jewellery), including nets made of faience disc beads, cartouches with the king's name, beads with Hathor faces and dangling floral pendants. Taharqo established a new royal cemetery at Nuri, about 25 kilometres (15½ mi.) upstream of el-Kurru, where all his Napatan successors would be buried, except for Tanwetamani, who was buried in the ancestral cemetery.

A return to Nubia: Napatan period

Following the collapse of the double kingdom of Nubia and Egypt, successors to the kings of the Egyptian Dynasty 25 continued to rule at Napata. The reigns of the first two Napatan rulers, Atlanersa and Senkamanisken, continued the traditions of their predecessors while also beginning a reinterpretation of Egyptian customs and iconography to reflect native Nubian ideologies. Extensive building projects have not been dated to their reigns, but temple B700 located at the base of the Pure Mountain was started by Atlanersa and completed by Senkamanisken. At this time the royal burial ground at Nuri was reopened.

The reign of Anlamani, possibly the son of Senkamanisken, dates to the late seventh century BC. His enthronement stela has the first known mention of conflict with the ancestors of the modern Beja peoples, the Blemmyes:

> His Majesty caused his army to invade the foreign country Bulahau (Eastern Desert region to the Red Sea), the chief (that is, friend) of His Majesty being the commander thereof . . .
> A great blood bath was made among them, the number thereof

(of the dead) being unknown. [Then] they (the soldiers) [seized] four men, and they were brought as living captives. They (the soldiers) gained control of all their women, all their children, [all] their small cattle, and all their property.[13]

This conflict, whether actual or ceremonial for the enthronement rites, shows the continued ideology of victory over chaos and a return to calm organization.

Anlamani made additions to the palace at Napata (B1200) that had been first constructed by Piye.[14] He added inscribed door jambs to room B1234 that emphasize the ceremonial nature of this space. He also constructed the early Amun temple at Meroe. Following his death and burial at Nuri, his brother Aspelta ascended to the throne. His reign showed a continued effort to combine and reinterpret Egyptian ideology into a more Nubian mindset. He made further modifications to the palace at Napata by adding a series of rooms, designated as the 'New Year's Hall', where rites for the New Year probably took place, again highlighting the ceremonial elements of these rooms.

Conflict with Egypt occurred during his reign when Psamtik II campaigned into Nubia in 593 BC. A circular temple at Dokki Gel was destroyed by fire during the military incursions of Psamtik II and rebuilt in the reign of Aspelta. At Napata, broken statues were buried in temples B500 and B900, possibly suggesting the destruction of the Amun temple by Psamtik II and his army.[15] However, the actual occurrence of these events is questionable since, according to a stela from Tanis dating to the reign of Psamtik II, the site of Trgb was the southernmost point reached by his campaign because 'the river did not allow [it]'. This probably referred to the area of the Dongola Reach where the Nile changes course, thereby preventing ships from continuing since from here they would have had to travel upstream against the wind.[16] Furthermore, stelae at Shellal and Karnak mention Pnubs, probably Kerma, as the southernmost point that the Egyptians travelled into Nubia.[17] Regardless, the destruction of the Amun temple at Napata by the Egyptian army probably did not happen as neither stela mentions a victory of that magnitude against the Nubians.[18]

Following Aspelta's reign, ten rulers have been identified, but there are no surviving monumental royal inscriptions detailing approximately the next 150 years. During this time the royal cemetery remained at Nuri with the kings and queens buried in pyramid tombs. The kings continued to travel to sites throughout Nubia and give offerings to the god Amun at his various temples. Nubia was still known on the world stage during this time. Cambyses established a military base at Elephantine and arranged an invasion of Nubia (*c.* 525–522 BC) that was ultimately abandoned, as documented by Herodotus (III.17–25). Nubians as tribute bearers are represented on the reliefs of the Apadana, or audience hall, at Persepolis, bringing items such as elephant tusks and African animals to the kings of Persia.[19]

Irike-Amannote ascended to the throne following the death of his uncle Talakhamani in the second half of the fifth century BC. At this time the Persians had conquered Egypt and the Egyptians were revolting against their rule. This provided an opportunity for the Nubians to travel northwards and reclaim the First and Second Cataract regions. Conflicts with nomadic groups occurred around the time of his coronation yet they appear to have been subdued and the recaptured lands were dedicated to the Temple of Amun of Pnubs (Kerma). Although little archaeological and textual information remains from his reign, it appears that Irike-Amannote set into motion the rise of Nubian power, which would reach a peak during the Meroitic period (*c.* 300 BC–AD 350).

Royal legitimacy might have been called into question when Harsiyotef succeeded Baskakeren in the first half to the middle of the fourth century BC. Harsiyotef's 35-year reign was occupied by nine military victories, lavish donations to Amun, and temple-building projects at Napata, Meroe and Kawa. Following the reigns of two further kings, Nastañeñ assumed the throne in the last third of the fourth century BC. Both Harsiyotef and Nastañeñ claimed lineage from the founder of the Napatan line, Alara, possibly to strengthen their claims to the throne. Nastañeñ also participated in military campaigns to subdue the rising power of local rulers in Lower Nubia as well as desert nomad incursions. Five rulers reigned after the death of Nastañeñ. They would bring the Napatan period to a close.

Statuette of a Kushite king dating to Dynasty 25.

Emulating Egypt

Due to the Nubians' familiarity with Egyptian customs and religion, the Napatan rulers integrated Egyptian imagery from earlier periods into their statues. This is known as 'archaizing' and was used by the Nubian rulers to legitimize their control over Egypt. The use of Egyptian iconography may have also eased their rule of Egypt since they were showing themselves as Egyptians rather than as foreigners.

When the Nubian kings ascended to the throne, they adopted Egyptian-style titularies, the grouping of five names, four of which the king assumed following his coronation. These included the Horus Name, Two Ladies (*nebty*) Name, Golden Horus Name, the King of Upper and Lower Egypt (*nesu-bity*) Name, and their Son of Ra (birth) Name.

By the reign of Kashta the king was already declaring himself to be the 'King of Upper and Lower Egypt', and had also adopted the 'Son of Ra' element of the titulary. Piye was the first Kushite king to adopt the full Egyptian titulary. His Two Ladies and Golden Horus names were modelled after the Egyptian king Thutmose III and his Horus name, 'Strong-bull, Appearing-in-Napata', was a direct reference to Thutmose III's Horus name, 'Strong-bull, Appearing-in-Thebes'.

With the introduction of the Meroitic script, beginning in the late second century BC, the rulers abandoned the traditional five-part titulary. The beginning of the Meroitic period also saw a new dynastic line emerging. When Arkamaniqo, a contemporary of Ptolemy II (282–246 BC), developed his titulary, he chose the throne name of Amasis of Dynasty 26 (570–526 BC): 'The Heart of Ra Rejoices'. Amasis took the throne of Egypt by force when he deposed his predecessor, Apries. Since Arkamaniqo chose to model his titulary after the usurper Amasis rather than the kings of the New Kingdom, he may have been admitting to taking the throne by force as well.

As the Nubian kings solidified their rulership, they began to incorporate more indigenous iconography into their representations on monuments. Headdresses worn by the Napatan kings and

queens were a mixture of Egyptian-influenced regalia and traditional Nubian regalia. The Egyptian White and Red Crowns,
which symbolized dominion over both Upper and Lower Egypt,
could be used interchangeably by the Nubian rulers with their
own headdresses. However, this dual imagery disappeared from
Egyptian royal iconography when the Nubians withdrew from
Egypt.

The most prominent Nubian headdress was a skullcap that
fitted to the head, sat low on the forehead and contained a diadem,
with one or two uraeus serpents at the brow and streamers hanging
down the back. This headdress was substituted for the Egyptian
Double Crown in the Napatan period. Over time the Nubian kings
and queens adapted the headdresses to accommodate their ideology. During the reign of King Natakamani and Queen Amanitore
in the second half of the first century AD, the serpent head on the
uraeus was replaced by a lion head. This modification is probably
due to the increased importance of the lion-headed god Apedemak
during the later Meroitic period.

Beginning of a new era

In the third century BC the capital moved further south to Meroe.
Evidence of occupation at Meroe pre-dates the shift of the capital's location, but it remains unclear who was living there or the
purpose of the site. A rubbish pit contained numerous objects
including faience sistra and *ankh*-signs presented to Amun at the
New Year. Inscribed rings bearing the names of the Napatan rulers
Aspelta, Aramatelqo, Malonaqen and Si'aspiqo date the pit to the
earlier building phase from approximately the eighth to the early
fifth centuries BC.[20]

The Western Cemetery at Meroe was established during the
mid-eighth century BC and was used by members of an elite class.
The Southern Cemetery, an elite and royal burial ground, was also
established prior to the capital shift in the third century BC. The
reason for moving the capital is unknown, although it is possible
that a new dynastic line, which originated in the south, decided
to relocate to their ancestral region. The burial of King Arkamani

(*c.* 270–260 BC) in the South Cemetery at Meroe provides a ten-tative date for the establishment of the Meroitic capital in the third century BC. This king has been equated with the Hellenistic Ergamenes who lived at the same time as Ptolemy II of Egypt. King Amanitikha eventually moved the royal burial ground and established the Northern Cemetery, which would remain in use for the duration of the Meroitic period.

During the Meroitic period the Nubian rulers began a coun-trywide building campaign which included temples, tombs and palaces. The development of the settlement at Meroe is still uncer-tain. A large enclosure wall (*c.* 8 hectares/19.8 acres) surrounds the Royal City, encompassing a series of palatial buildings. The Amun temple is located to the east of this enclosure and has sev-eral small shrines nearby. Two large mounds are located outside the enclosure to the northeast and south, known as the 'North Mound' and the 'South Mound', respectively. Additional areas surrounding the Royal City include industrial sectors for pot-tery and iron production and the so-called 'Isis Temple' and 'Sun Temple'. The remains of non-royal settlement areas have yet to be excavated.

Palace M750, located outside the Royal City walls, is a curious composite building. It was built of mud-brick on a foundation of dressed sandstone blocks from earlier buildings. Many of the blocks have incised reliefs or architectural carvings demonstrating a range of sizes, styles and themes. Large, well-preserved cornice blocks with uraei and star friezes were found in the foundation layers along the main axis, indicating that they came from care-fully dismantled edifices. Some of the blocks date to the late first century AD into the second, thus providing a tentative date for the building's construction.

M750 appears to have consisted of two parts connected by a courtyard. The northern portion of the building featured a monumental pylon entrance facing north, oriented towards the processional way leading to the Amun Temple M260. The rooms were symmetrically arranged along the eastern and western sides of the building with a columned courtyard in the middle. The south-ern portion of the building was square in shape, and also arranged

North Cemetery at Meroe.

around a central courtyard. While the southern portion has generally been accepted as the residential sector for the building, it remains unclear whether the northern portion of the palace served as the administrative sector or, owing to the monumental pylon, if it was a temple. The possible need for a royal temple attached to the palace could suggest a strong, personal connection with the deity.

To the south of the capital at the site of Wad ban Naga is a palace attributed to Queen Amanishakheto, who ruled Nubia during the late first century BC. Her palace has the remains of ramps, staircases and composite column capitals, indicating the presence of a second storey. This building also has a large quantity of storerooms which suggests that the queen needed to provide for a sizeable staff, palace workshops and the royal family. Luxury items such as a decorated silver ring were discovered in the storerooms. Silver was a precious metal imported by Meroitic rulers from the Graeco-Roman world.

Meroe and its neighbours

The Meroitic rulers controlled Nubia for approximately six hundred years, where they traded commodities with their neighbours to the north and across the Red Sea. Contact between the Meroitic Empire and the Mediterranean world began with the conquest of Egypt by Alexander the Great in 332 BC. The subsequent Ptolemaic period brought Greek language and elements of Greek culture to Egypt. These aspects were eventually transferred to Nubia, where Greek was probably understood and used by the ruling and merchant classes of both countries.[21]

The construction of the famed Library of Alexandria was begun by Ptolemy I (305–282 BC). His son Ptolemy II expanded the library and enhanced trade throughout the Mediterranean and down the Red Sea coast, including stops at Meroitic ports to acquire military elephants.[22] These initial connections between Hellenistic Egypt and Meroitic Nubia eventually evolved into Greeks travelling to and living at Meroe, thereby bringing their own culture and ideas to Nubia.

The Nubian rulers reclaimed Lower Nubia following a rebellion sometime between 207/206 and 186 BC. After this event the area was administered by a local governor ('peshto') who reported directly to the king. The residence of the peshto was located first at Faras and later at Karanog, where a large residence, called a 'castle' by early archaeologists, was built.

Following the conquest of Egypt by Rome, contact between Roman Egypt and Nubia continued from the first century BC to the early third century AD. During this time the two cultures shared a common frontier, known as the Dodecaschoenus, which stretched 120 kilometres (74½ mi.) south of Aswan to el-Maharraqa in Nubia. As with contact between Nubia and Egypt, and later with the Ptolemies, relations with Rome occurred primarily in Lower Nubia. In 30 BC, Caius Cornelius Gallus, the new Prefect of Egypt selected by Augustus, appointed a Roman client ruler, or *tyrannos*, for the Triacontaschoenus, a 'buffer zone' between Nubia and Egypt. After this appointment Gallus required the local Meroitic rulers to declare Roman suzerainty and pay tribute to Rome.[23] On a trilingual stela found at the Temple of Augustus at Philae, Gallus fashioned himself as a 'public friend' to the Meroitic ruler.[24]

However, a war between Meroe and Rome broke out shortly after. The Nubians in the region of the Triacontaschoenus rebelled against the heavy taxation imposed by Rome by invading and vandalizing the Egyptian areas of Syene, Elephantine and Philae.[25] In order to provide support to the rebels, the Meroitic king Teriteqas set out on a campaign with his troops. Unfortunately, in the autumn of 25 BC the king died after reaching Dakka. His successor, Queen Amanirenas, assumed command of the army and began negotiations with Rome.[26] As peace negotiations continued, the newly appointed third Roman Prefect of Egypt, Caius Petronius, set off for Nubia in the direction of Napata. He later returned to Egypt with spoils, although he did not succeed in his attempted takeover. The result of the mediation between Meroe and Rome was the Treaty of Samos, drafted in 21 BC. Under this treaty peace prevailed: Nubian pilgrims journeyed to the temple at Philae and Roman goods, such as amphorae, jewellery and household furnishings, were imported into Nubia. Many such objects were discovered at royal and elite residential buildings and funerary sites, indicating the objects were gift exchanges by way of diplomatic relations between the two powers.[27]

Nubian architecture incorporated Mediterranean imagery. One of the most notable examples is the Royal Bath or Water Sanctuary at Meroe. The Water Sanctuary consists of a deep basin with stairs leading into it from the southeast corner. The decorative programme shows a mixture of Nubian, Egyptian and Mediterranean imagery. Around the upper portion of the basin are carved sandstone lion- and bull-headed figures painted with polychromy. Along with the heads, there were medallions with *ankhs* (the symbol for life) and protection signs, medallions with just an *ankh*, inlays of Apedemak on the crescent moon, and reliefs showing female busts, all made of faience. Above this series of sculptures and reliefs were paintings depicting elephants marching to the right.

In addition to the decorative elements found along the upper level of the basin, a collection of less than life-size sandstone statues

Decoration in water sanctuary at Meroe.

and column drums was discovered within the water sanctuary. These statues had characteristics that were similar to Hellenistic statuary, such as short, straight locks of hair combed towards the forehead and surmounted with a broad fillet, and figures shown drinking from a shared vessel, a common element in Greek and Etruscan funerary monuments.

The so-called 'Roman Kiosk' at Naqa demonstrates the influence of the Mediterranean world on Meroitic religious architecture. The kiosk has T-shaped pillars along with engaged half-columns.[28] The lintels atop the doorways show three layers of winged sun discs along with an uraeus serpent on either side of the disc. On the uppermost level of the lintel is a line of uraei with a sun disc atop their heads, reminiscent of Egyptian architectural elements and themes. While the main doorways were decorated with purely Egyptian-style iconography, the windows were arched, making them indicative of Roman window design. The pillars and engaged columns have unadorned bases and shafts as seen on Roman-style columns. Two types of capitals were used in the kiosk. The first was a composite capital with flaring vegetation at the top found on the eight half-columns of the four corners. The second type used was an Alexandrian Corinthian capital, again with flaring vegetation and a collar of acanthus leaves, a characteristic of late Hellenistic Alexandrian capitals.[29]

Greek-style architecture continued to be in vogue during the reigns of Natakamani and Amanitore in the second half of the first century AD. Their palace at Napata (B1500) was decorated with elements that were fashionable at the time. The column capitals recovered at the exterior of the building were ornately decorated and reminiscent of Greek Corinthian columns. Conversely, the columns found in the interior of the building had papyri-form capitals, similar to those in Egyptian monuments. The arrangement of the interior columns suggested a peristyle hall located on two floors as seen in Hellenistic exterior facades.[30]

The exterior faience decoration, discovered scattered around the perimeter of the building, also showed signs of Hellenistic motifs. Medallions appear to have been placed at a certain height in an alternating pattern of a lion, possibly Apedemak, grasping a crescent moon and floral decoration with a combination of incised life and protection signs, similar to the Water Sanctuary at Meroe.

Roman 'kiosk' at Naqa.

Other medallions discovered had representations of feminine busts carved in raised relief. The figures' faces are slightly raised towards either shoulder, with the eyes looking upwards and the hair shown in heavy curls which are held in place with a crown that is suggestive of Alexandrian statuary.[31]

Along with their Mediterranean connections, the Meroitic rulers continued contact with the Aksumite kingdom, an area of ancient Ethiopia located within the Tigrai region, stretching from near the base of the Adwa mountains to the Akkele Guzai in ancient Eritrea. Early contact with Nubia, particularly the area of Kassala in eastern Sudan, and the Aksumite region is tentative. However, the presence of some small finds may indicate a developing relationship. At the cemetery of Ona Enda Aboi Zewgé (OAZ) a conical bronze seal inscribed with a crescent moon or sun disc was discovered in tomb 6. Both the crescent moon and sun disc are symbols found in South Arabian and Meroitic iconography.[32] The sites of Mahal Teglinos at Kassala and Kerma also had fired clay stamp seals with geometric designs that were probably used for communication between the two sites.[33] The presence of foreign ceramic fragments indicates that Mahal Teglinos was an integral component within the complex network of connections spanning Egypt and Nubia to the Horn of Africa and southern Arabia.[34]

Subsidiary burials, potentially human sacrifices, were found at OAZ I and VII. The bodies from both burials had minimal grave goods and were non-intrusive. These burials may have served a purpose similar to that of the subsidiary burials from the Kerma Classique (c. 1750–1450 BC). Burials of this type were also found in a Late Meroitic tomb at West Meroe and at Ballana and Qustul.[35] These finds in Nubian elite burials suggest symbolic behaviour also found in elite Proto-Aksumite (c. 384–32 BC) burials, which may indicate the widespread dispersion of certain funerary symbols from Nubia to Ethiopia/Eritrea in addition to contact between Upper Nubia and Ethiopia/Eritrea during the Proto-Aksumite period.

The site of Yeha, located in Tigrai in northern Ethiopia, approximately 25 kilometres (15½ mi.) northeast of the modern town of Adwa, has a large settlement consisting of two monumental temples and a cemetery. The shaft-tombs contained an abundance of luxury goods, including items imported from Nubia, and the only occurrence of zoomorphic (animal form) bronze seals with personal names.[36]

Contact between Nubia and the Aksumite region is also evident from a carnelian amulet of Harpocrates with a necklace and double uraeus, a characteristic of the Meroitic kings, found at Matara, Eritrea.[37] At Addi Galamo there were four bronze cups discovered in a hole that also contained southern Arabian and Aksumite objects. Two of these cups were decorated with engraved figures such as frogs on papyrus on the outside, as well as bulls and a rosette on the inside. In addition to the Nubian artefacts found in Ethiopia/Eritrea, the remains of an Aksumite throne were found in Nubia at the confluence of the Nile and Atbara rivers, undeniable evidence of Aksumite–Nubian contact.

The transfer of goods and ideas between the Arabian Peninsula, the Aksumite Empire and the Meroitic Empire may be due to a group of professional Sabean tradesmen known as *grbyn*.[38] These tradesmen travelled from the Arabian Peninsula into the Abyssinian highlands and potentially into Meroitic Nubia. They were also considered to be highly qualified builders, architects and urban planners, and were awarded high status in the kingdom of Sheba, a polity centred in northwestern Yemen.

The Great Enclosure at Musawwarat es-Sufra is unquestionably one of the most distinctive buildings in Nubia. It has a clear religious function evidenced by images of deities, in particular the god Apedemak, throughout the building. The most interesting thing about the Great Enclosure is its design, as there are no parallels within Nubia or any of its surrounding areas. However, this structure may be the culmination of the amalgamation of multiple cultures influencing a single building. The design of the Great Enclosure is not linear, as would be expected from Egyptian, Nubian, Greek or Roman religious buildings. Instead the central terrace is organized in a concentric fashion with vestibules and corridors leading off the main sanctuary and may have been influenced from contact with the Aksumite region.

This terraced layout can be found in buildings from the Aksumite region such as the Palace of Dungur in Ethiopia and the palatial elements of structures B, C and D at Matara. These buildings have an approximately square plan for the main central building, set within an overall concentric layout. The areas extending from the central portion of the building would have been connected via ramps or gradual staircases as in the Great Enclosure. Although the buildings at Dungur and Matara postdate the Great Enclosure, this type of architecture was presumably used for large-scale sacred and secular architecture prior to these two buildings. Unfortunately, Proto-Aksumite palaces have never been extensively published and any earlier buildings at Dungur and Matara have yet to be excavated.

Language and arts

One of the most important developments during the Meroitic period was the adoption of the Meroitic language and script as the official state language of communication. Until this point Egyptian hieroglyphs had been used as the primary written form of communication throughout the New Kingdom colonization and remained in use by the Egyptian Dynasty 25 and Napatan rulers, whose monumental stelae were composed using Classical Middle Egyptian. The development of the Meroitic hieroglyphic and cursive scripts occurred sometime during the second century BC and these were used by royals and non-royals alike. Although written Meroitic was not employed until the new capital had already been established, a spoken version of the language was probably already in use as early as the first millennium BC, as may be seen in name components. The Meroitic form of the god Amun was read as *amani* rather than the Egyptian *'Imn*. Kings and queens incorporated this version of the god's name into their own, for example Tanwetamani, Talakhamani, Amanishakheto and Amanitore. Kashta means 'The Kushite' in Meroitic, and other words such as *mak* (god), *malo* (good) and *mote* (child) were elements of royal and non-royal names.[39]

Written Meroitic appeared quite suddenly and its first known use, dating to the reign of Queen Shanadakheto (second half of the second century BC), was found at Naqa. The language consists of Egyptian signs that functioned as syllables matching the new language, rather than being copies of the original. Early inscriptions on official stelae were probably read out to the non-literate public, who could immediately understand the contents since the language being used was their native tongue. Unlike Egyptian, the Meroitic script uses two or three vertical dots to divide words. This certainly would have made it easier for a non-native learner of the language who might not have an extensive vocabulary.

The Meroitic scripts were used in both religious and secular contexts and range from inscriptions on small objects to large temple inscriptions. Although great strides have been made to decipher the language and some personal names, toponyms and titles are able to be read, it unfortunately remains largely untranslatable.[40] If the texts are similar to those from earlier periods, they most likely include records of political achievements, temple donations and mortuary offerings.

Along with the Meroitic language, a new type of pottery was developed during this time which can be recognized from its intricate patterns and high production quality. Representations of animals (such as cattle, giraffes, frogs and ostriches), human figures (including those engaging in pastoral activities, bound prisoners, dancing fauns and satyrs), and types of flora such as sorghum and vine scrolls were depicted on the pottery. Abundant examples of this pottery have been found in Lower Nubia, particularly at Faras and Karanog. Later Meroitic period workshops producing this fine ware have been found at Musawwarat es-Sufra and Meroe, indicating that the pottery was valued and used throughout the country.

End of an empire

All empires rise and fall, and the Meroitic Empire came to an end in the fourth century AD. Given that Meroe was located at the intersection of five main trade routes – the Nile route, which lies along the Blue and White Niles, the Butana route, the Sinkat pass route, the Bayuda route and the Korosko route – Meroitic rulers

Votive plaque of the Meroitic ruler King Tanyidamani, with a Meroitic inscription giving the name of the king and the god Apedemak.

Collection of Meroitic pottery from Faras.

would have maintained control over trade along these paths to the African interior. Yeha, however, was located at the intersection of five other trade routes – two from the Sudanese lowlands, one from Western Ethiopia and two along the Red Sea – which would have provided the Aksumite rulers with control over trade along the Red Sea coast. Rivalry between the rulers of Meroe and Aksum to control all the routes leading into the African interior would have been inevitable.

Two Greek inscriptions of a king of Aksum dating to the third or fourth century AD found at Meroe describe conflicts between the Meroitic and Aksumite kingdoms.[41] These texts probably pre-date the reign of Ezana, the first Christian king of Aksum, indicating growing tensions between the two empires. Unfortunately, they are both rather fragmented so few details can be gleaned from them.

Ezana invaded Meroe sometime in the mid-fourth century AD. While there has been debate as to the exact nature of Ezana's campaign and the fall of Meroe, the presence of Greek victory inscriptions naming Ezana as the king of Aithiopians (that is, Nubians) and Kasu (Meroe) is strongly suggestive of his conquest.[42]

The end of the Meroitic Empire was marked by the rise of powerful elite groups, as can be seen from their lavish burials in the Western Cemetery. Over time the capital was abandoned and the temples eventually fell into disuse. The last dated Meroitic ruler was King Teqorideamani (AD 253). The abandonment of Meroe caused another period of transition for the country during which smaller power bases replaced centralized government.

FIVE

THE NUBIAN
PANTHEON

Prior to the New Kingdom colonization (*c.* 1550–1070 BC), an indigenous religion was practised in Nubia in which hilltops, caves and rocky outcrops were sacred. A belief in the afterlife at early periods of their history is evident from grave goods discovered at various cemetery sites. Information about Nubian religious practices mainly comes from elite and royal contexts, since such sources are better preserved.

The construction of the Western Deffufa at the city of Kerma and the Eastern Deffufa at the associated royal cemetery marks the first known permanent religious structures in Nubia. During the Egyptian colonization, free-standing temples, dedicated to Egyptian deities and rulers, were built along the Nile to the Fourth Cataract region. With the prevalence of these temples, Nubians began worshipping the Egyptian gods and goddess. They also started incorporating Egyptian deities into their pantheon as well as attributing to them aspects of their own Nubian gods and goddesses.

It is clear that animals played an important role in Nubian religious ideology. The Egyptian god Amun was one of the most important deities in the Nubian pantheon. His importance began to flourish during the New Kingdom colonization but the roots for his acceptance as a powerful deity may possibly be found in the Kerma period. Representations of the god in Nubia incorporated indigenous belief systems showing Amun as a ram or a ram-headed man rather than in the Egyptian style of a human-headed man wearing a headdress with tall plumes. The ram cult was established in Nubia as early as the Kerma period when rams, adorned with decorated sun discs, ostrich feathers and ivory horn protectors, were buried as offerings to the dead. New Kingdom and later Nubian kings started adding Amun's curved horns to their headdresses, illustrative of Amun's new status.

The Nubians' ancestral belief that natural formations had religious significance enabled Napata to be recognized as an important site. The landscape centres around a flat-topped mountain, called 'Pure Mountain' in ancient times, that was believed to be the dwelling place of Amun in Nubia. During the reign of Piye, the Amun cult was restored throughout Nubia, especially at the sites of Napata, Kawa and Pnubs (Kerma). The construction of a

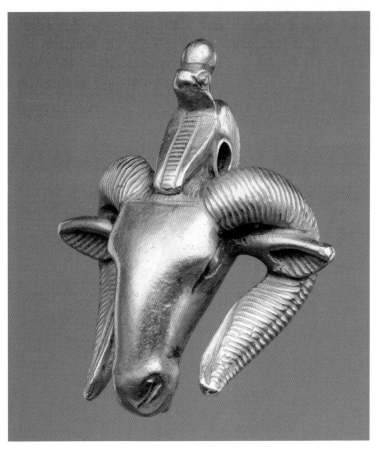

Ram's head amulet pendant of the god Amun-Ra dating to Dynasty 25.

Pure Mountain at Napata (Jebel Barkal).

temple dedicated to Amun at Napata (B500) marked a significant development for the god's cult and most of the temples built were dedicated to him.[1] This provided a connection for the veneration of the god in both Nubia and Egypt, marking Napata as the Nubian counterpart to Karnak and the southern home of the deity.

In the New Kingdom the ram-headed Amun of Nubia was syncretized with the ram-headed god Khnum of Elephantine.[2] Khnum controlled the annual inundation of the Nile, so their connection allowed Amun to assume this role as well. The New Kingdom pharaoh Thutmose III constructed a temple at Elephantine dedicated to Amun, who was worshipped along with members of Khnum's divine triad, Satis and Anukis. It is possible that the Egyptians combined Amun with the Nubian ram-headed god to strengthen their control over Nubia by providing the Nubians with a bringer of the inundation.[3] The official New Year began when the Nile started to rise. The ceremonies performed at this time were focused on the renewal of life and fertility for all of Egypt and Nubia. The importance of the king's participation in the New Year's festival activities is found in various textual sources from Dynasty 25 (*c.* 760–656 BC) and the Napatan period (*c.* 800–300 BC).

In the Great Triumphal Stela of Piye, the king coordinated his campaign with the inundation:

> I shall sail north myself . . . After the ceremonies of the New Year have been performed, I shall offer to my father Amun on his beautiful festival, when he makes his beautiful appearance of the New Year that he may send me in peace to see Amun in the beautiful festival of the Feast of Opet.[4]

This gave his expedition religious significance since he conquered Egypt from the south to the north, in the same manner as the course of the Nile.

When Tanwetamani made his campaign to Egypt in 664/663 BC he followed a similar path and timeline, thereby joining the sacred landscapes of Nubia and Egypt once again:

> His Majesty went to Napata . . . North sailed His Majesty to North-land . . . There arrived His Majesty at Elephantine . . . Then His Majesty sailed across to Elephantine. There he came to the temple-compound of Khnum-Re, lord of the Cataract . . . North went His Majesty to the city, Thebes of Amûn . . . North sailed His Majesty . . . There arrived His Majesty at Memphis.[5]

The idea of Amun being the bringer of the inundation continued into the late phases of the Napatan period when Harsiyotef was given the crown by Amun of Napata, who then also gave the new king the inundation:

> To you is given the crown of the land of Nubia. I give to you the 4 corners of the land in its entirety. (I) give to you the good water (that is, the inundation). (I) give you a sky of good rain . . . Now I saw a great Inundation which Amun, my good father, gave to me.[6]

The Nile was also an important means for purification for both buildings and people before and during religious ceremonies. The ritual of purifying the new pharaoh with water did not necessarily occur at the same time as the coronation ceremonies, but it did have a connection with the accession of the new king since it was an important element in establishing his royal power.

During the Napatan period there was a connection between water and the divine nature of Napata. A graffito on the mountain shows a ram-headed snake with the upraised arm of Kamutef. Here, Amun's power is represented as a liquid being poured from the interior of the mountain, symbolizing the king's ability to unite the kingdom. Amun of Napata was recognized as the provider of universal power, which emphasizes both water as a purifier and royal legitimacy.[7] This tradition continued into the Meroitic period (c. 300 BC–AD 350). Potsherds from building B2200 were discovered during excavations there bearing a variety of motifs including Egyptian religious, Hellenistic and local themes. The Egyptian motifs mainly consisted of *ankh* and lotus flowers, with one having a representation of Hathor and offering tables. This type of pottery decoration can be found on Meroitic funerary vessels along with representations of frogs. The imagery of frogs and lotus flowers are symbols of rebirth and eternal life along with their association with the life-giving power of the Nile.[8] A serpent motif, representing Amun as the god Kamutef, as well as a serpent with vine leaves emerging from it are combinations of Egyptian and Hellenistic religious motifs of chthonic powers and rebirth.

Evidence for the king's purification can be found in Napatan and Meroitic period temples. The Amun Temple at Meroe (M260) featured a shallow square basin in the centre of the hypostyle hall that was used as the site of the king's purification in the temple at the time of his coronation. Temple T at Kawa has a scene of the purification of Taharqo located on the north wall of the forecourt. Here, the king is being purified by Horus and Thoth, who are shown as participants in the king's coronation. Following his purification and coronation, Taharqo is then brought into the presence of Amun of Kawa, thereby completing his enthronement ceremony.

Due to astronomical markings and Early Meroitic cursive graffiti containing calculations, it was suggested that the sandstone basins discovered under building M950 in room complex M954 and M954a at Meroe were part of an 'observatory'.[9] The astronomical markings and calculations might have been used to determine the hours of the day and night, thus measuring the seasons, and identifying the date of the inundation. These basins may have been used to store pure water from the inundation, which could be used during religious ceremonies throughout the year. This was a common practice in temples and private houses in Hellenistic and Roman Egypt, which was then transferred to Nubia.[10]

Divine legitimization of the king

The notion of a divinely chosen king was recognized by the Nubian rulers, yet whether it existed prior to contact with Egypt is uncertain. Nubian rulers were interested in aspects of Egyptian kingship philosophy because in Nubia there were more conflicts and choices associated with succession than in Egypt.

Amun's importance to the Nubian kings was also documented in inscriptions found on stelae and temple walls. The unnamed king in the inscription of Katimalo states, 'I having not called to mind the event that happened to me in this year, when Amun nodded his approval (in an oracle) for (my) [accession].'[11] On the Election Stela of Aspelta, Amun is venerated as the original god of Nubia who would choose the next king: 'He (Amun) has been the god of the king of Kush since the time of Re. It is he that guides us. The kings of Kush have (always) been in his hands. He has (always) given (it) to (his) son whom he loves.'[12] The presence of the manifestations of Amun at Napata, Kawa and Pnubs indicates that the ancient cults of the local forms of the god were re-established and their importance increased.[13]

In addition to having their reigns legitimized by Amun, the Nubian kings also believed in the maintenance of *ma'at*, the Egyptian concept of cosmic harmony. At the time of their coronation, the kings strove to re-establish *ma'at* through the rebuilding of temples, military activities and providing donations to the priesthood and temples. Taharqo was particularly avid in this endeavour and rebuilt temples at former New Kingdom period centres such as the Temple of Horus of Mi'am at Faras, the Temple of Horus of Buhen at Buhen, and the Temple of the deified Senwosret III and Dedwen at Semna West.[14] The temples at Dokki Gel were also rebuilt during the reign of Irike-Amannote.[15]

The ideal coronation ceremony took place in conjunction with the first day of the inundation, which was witnessed through the re-emergence of the New Kingdom Nubian Amuns. Although the coronation of the new king was intended to coincide with the New Year, the need to appoint a successor and crown him could not always be arranged around the calendrical dates.[16] Therefore the new king would be crowned, and when the New Year followed, a jubilee with renewal rites would be performed.

One of the few examples of the coronation ceremonies performed by the Egyptians that can be equated with the Nubians is the account of the coronation of King Horemheb (c. 1323–1295 BC).[17] Since Horemheb was not a member of the royal family, he also had to affirm his claim to the throne through the support of the gods. In an attempt to legitimize his claim, Horemheb stated that he had possessed kingly qualities since birth as he was born with his body clothed in majesty. The coronation ceremony was held in Thebes where Amun bestowed upon him the office of kingship.

When Horemheb was crowned by Amun-Ra he was listed as being in the *per nesu* (palace), which is a term generally not applied to a temple.[18] Horemheb instead went to the *per wer* (great house) of Amun's daughter and received her (that is, the uraeus) on his forehead as the gods of the *per neser* (house of flame) shouted joyfully.

The *per wer* was typically associated with Nekhbet, the vulture goddess of the White Crown of Upper Egypt, and the *per neser* was associated with Wadjet, the cobra goddess of the Red Crown of Lower Egypt. These places were the shrines visited by the Egyptian kings during their coronation ceremonies in order to receive their emblems of kingship.[19] By the reign of Horemheb they were rooms visited within the Temple of Karnak at Thebes rather than the traditional temples at the sites of el-Kab in the south and Buto in the Delta.

Door jambs found in room B1234 of palace B1200 at Napata bear inscriptions that date to the reign of Anlamani (late seventh century BC). These inscriptions also indicate that even Nubian kings went into the *per wer* and *per neser* of the temple during their coronation ceremonies. It was in these rooms that the king received his crowns.

Sometimes dreams were used as a means to legitimize a ruler's reign. On the Dream Stela of Tanwetamani, he recounts a dream he had where Amun granted him the crown:

> His Majesty saw a dream in the night, two serpents, one on his right, the other on his left. Up woke His Majesty but did not find them. His Majesty said, 'Why has this happened to me?' Then reply was made to him, saying, 'South-land (Nubia) is yours (already), (now) seize for yourself North-land (Egypt). The Two-Ladies are apparent on your head, and the land shall be given to you in its breadth and its length, there being none other that shall share (it) with you.'[20]

The fact that Tanwetamani later had a stela erected detailing his enthronement indicates this dream occurred before his coronation ceremonies. The use of dreams as a form of legitimization can also be seen in the reign of Harsiyotef (early fourth century BC), who wanted to reinforce his place as heir to Irike-Amannote (second half of fifth century BC). In the Annals of Harsiyotef, the king recounts the god's words throughout the country:

> I went to Amen-Rê, the lord dwelling in Finding-(the-) Aton (Kawa), and told about what Amûn of Napata said to me. I went to Amen-Rê, the lord dwelling in Pnubs (Kerma) and told about what Amûn of Napata said. I went to Bastet of Tare and told about what Amûn of Napata said.[21]

By visiting these sites and proclaiming what Amun of Napata had said, Harsiyotef was reaffirming his right to the throne.

The coronation procedure during the Napatan period was more complicated than simply allowing the king's son and heir apparent to ascend the throne. The process of selecting a new ruler was documented in royal inscriptions such as the Election Stela of Aspelta (end of the seventh century BC) and the Inscription of Irike-Amannote. In both accounts, the new king was in the palace with the army gathered following the death of the previous king:

> Now there were trusted commanders in the midst of His Majesty's (Aspelta's) army . . . they said to the entire army, 'Come, let us cause our lord to appear.'[22]
>
> Then His Majesty's (Irike-Amannote) army together with the commanders of His Majesty's army went into the palace.[23]

After the king appeared, they would then either consult the oracle of Amun of Napata, 'Off went His Majesty's commanders and the "friends" of the palace to the temple-compound of Amun . . . They said to them (the priests), "O may this god Amen-Re . . . cause that he give us our lord (Aspelta)".'[24] Or, they would immediately name the chosen successor, 'Our (the army's) heart is (set) on giving him (Irike-Amannote) the throne [of] this [land].'[25]

Following the election, the newly appointed king would participate in the coronation ceremonies, which involved travelling to the sites of Meroe, Napata, Kawa and Kerma, where the local manifestation of Amun conferred royal power upon him. Performing the ceremonies at the different sites enabled the power of the king to be associated with the person rather than a specific location, particularly throughout the Dongola-Napata Reach.[26] Thus where the king was in residence was the seat of his authority.

The organization of Nubia was centred around an Amun temple–royal palace complex that enabled the land to be comprised of equal governmental units wherein each individual unit was a representation of the ideal whole of the land. This relationship between the temples and palaces has been identified based on the orientation of the royal residence to the axis of the Amun temple during the New Kingdom.[27]

The palace and temple facades both contain scenes of royal dominion over foreigners on columns and door jambs. The interior walls of the palaces probably had scenes of royal ceremonies that would have taken place within the building, as well as processions of troops out of the building. Similarly, temple scenes show ritual activity taking place within the temple walls along with processions traversing the court and leaving the temple. These connections indicate that the ceremonies associated with the king in the palace are similar to the authority displayed by the gods and their rituals in the temple.[28] This relationship between the palaces and Amun temples has been noted in sites across Nubia. The palaces were oriented in the same manner to the processional avenue of the associated Amun temple, since the king's movement in divine processions could be towards either the temple or the palace.

Along with the ceremonies at Meroe, Napata, Kawa and Kerma, the enthronement rites were sometimes performed in the Temple of Bastet at Tare, which differed from the pilgrimages to the Amun temples. The importance of honouring Bastet in the coronation ceremonies might have had its origin during the reign of Piye, since her name appears in his titulary as 'Son of Bastet' instead of the traditional 'Son of Ra'. The goddess's importance to the Nubian kings might be connected to the goddesses Mut, Sekhmet and Tefnut through their mutual association as the Eye of Ra, protectresses of the sun god. Perhaps in Nubia, Bastet also assumed that role, thereby establishing her temple at Tare as another location where the king would receive his royal crowns and uraei.

The practice continued throughout the Napatan period. The Stela of Nastaseñ (second half of the fourth century BC) also details the king's coronation route, which included a visit to Tare in addition to the primary coronation sites: '(I) went up to Bastet who dwells in Tele (Tare), my good mother. She gave (to) me life, a long beautiful old age, and (her) left breast.'[29] In both Egypt and Nubia milk was used in important rituals as a tool for rejuvenation and transformation, since the use of milk in a non-funerary context typically conferred divinity upon the recipient. The ritual of breastfeeding at the conclusion of the coronation ceremonies was already practised in Egypt during the New Kingdom, and a

Opposite: Menat of Bastet nursing Taharqo.

goddess nursing the king was a representation of the mother–son relationship that was an important element of the legitimization of the king. Through this act, the king was infused with the essence of royalty and brought into the divine realm.[30] The goddesses associated with nursing the king were Isis, Mut and Bastet. Isis was the quintessential mother goddess as the mother of Horus, the divine manifestation of the living king, and subsequently the mother of the king. On a silver plaque from the tomb of Queen Nefrukekashta at el-Kurru, a queen is shown being nursed by a goddess.[31] This was rare, yet it demonstrates the importance of women as life-givers and as strong counterparts to the king.

Meroitic religion

With the rise of the Meroitic Empire came a newfound emphasis on indigenous Nubian gods. The god Apedemak became one of the deities, if not the primary one, in the Meroitic pantheon. His name means 'the protector' and he is represented with a lion's head. He is often shown with a bow and arrow bringing prisoners to the ruler, emphasizing his role as a warrior and hunter.[32] The Lion Temple at Naqa, constructed by Natakamani and Amanitore (second half of the first century AD), provides us with several depictions of the god. On the sides of the pylons he is shown as a lion-headed serpent with human arms and hands wearing the elaborate *hem-hem* crown rising from a lotus. The walls of the temple show Apedemak as a lion-headed man, again wearing the *hem-hem* crown. In one instance he is depicted as a man with three lion heads and four human arms. A lion killing an enemy can also be found between the legs of Natakamani on the face of the pylon. His consort Amesemi is shown as a woman with a headdress comprised of a double falcon on a crescent.

The gods Arensnuphis and Sebiumeker, both warriors and hunters, were frequently shown together. They were guardians of temples and were often shown flanking temple entrances.[33] Sebiumeker, whose name means 'Lord of Musawwarat', is

Opposite: Serpent form of Apedemak at Naqa.

Lion Temple at Naqa.

represented as a man wearing a short kilt, the Egyptian Double Crown and a divine beard. Arensnuphis, whose name means 'the good companion', could be shown as a man wearing a short kilt, a crown of feathers and a divine beard, or as a lion. Along with the indigenous cults, the Meroitic people continued to worship the Egyptian deities Hathor, Isis, Osiris, Amun and Mut.

Meroitic coronation ceremonies

During the Meroitic period a change to kingship ideology occurred, reflecting the importance of the king as a warrior. The Great Enclosure at Musawwarat es-Sufra demonstrates this new ideology. On reliefs throughout this temple there were scenes of Apedemak actively participating in the coronation of the king.

Columns from Hall 101 of the Great Enclosure depict the indigenous as well as the new warrior iconography during the coronation ceremonies. In a scene on column 7 the prince, as the newly elected king, is shown wearing the Nubian cap-crown with diadem and a single uraeus as well as a ram's horn curled around his ear. The king's attire is the royal coat that fastened at the shoulder. He is being embraced by Horus on his left and Thoth on his right. Isis, located beside Horus, is shown giving the king the Red Crown of Lower Egypt.

A scene on column 8 shows Isis affirming the kingship by holding the ribbon hanging from the king's crown. The king and Isis stand before Sebiumeker. Between the king and the god is a lotus, from which emerges a winged cobra wearing the Double Crown of Egypt. The cobra extends its wings towards the newly elected king as a sign of protection. Another scene on column 8 shows the king before Apedemak and his consort Amesemi. Depicted between the king and the deities are bound captives attached to a rope held in the king's left hand, which is representational of Apedemak decreeing the king's power over his enemies.[34] The preserved scene on column 9 shows the king wearing his royal regalia and carrying a bow. He is being led by Arensnuphis to a ram-headed god who touches the king's right elbow. The Amun represented in this scene is probably Amun of Kawa, who traditionally bestows a bow on the king at his coronation.[35]

Two scenes on column 10 represent the final elements of the coronation ceremony. The left scene depicts the king, protected by a falcon above his head, before Apedemak. Behind the king is a prince, the heir apparent. Although the king would typically only receive his legitimization from the manifestations of Amun, the inclusion of the Meroitic gods indicates the increased importance of indigenous deities. The scene on the right shows the king facing Amun of Napata and Mut while wearing the crown of the hunter god Arensnuphis.[36] The king offers a pectoral to Amun, which represents the symbolic fulfilment of royal duties. Both deities in return offer *ankh*-signs, the symbol of life, to the king. Between the king and the deities is a winged cobra emerging from a lotus and wearing the Double Crown of Egypt and extending its wings toward the deities rather than the king. Given that this scene is intended to serve as the final element of the investiture of the new king and his association with Arensnuphis, the reverse direction of the winged cobra may be a representation of the king now being responsible for the protection of Nubia and the proper worship of the deities responsible for his legitimization.

Funerary religion

Napatan funerary beliefs and practices were also based on Egyptian models. The integration of Egyptian elements and their adaptation to native Nubian ideologies was most likely prompted by the emigration of Egyptians to Napata, particularly during the New Kingdom colonization and into the Napatan period. At this time, bodies were mummified and buried in coffins instead of being wrapped in a shroud and placed on funerary beds.[37] The deceased was equated with the god Osiris, the Egyptian god of death, resurrection and fertility, a long-held belief in Egyptian religion.

The Napatan kings incorporated elements of Egyptian-style texts, particularly those recorded on sarcophagi and stelae, into their funerary culture. Knowledge of these texts and their purposes was probably gained during the Nubian rule of Egypt during Dynasty 25, when a strong presence at Thebes, Egypt's religious capital, had been established. In 1918 George Reisner discovered the sarcophagi of Napatan kings Anlamani and Aspelta in the burial chambers of their pyramids at Nuri, numbers 6 and 8 respectively. Both sarcophagi were decorated with carved inscriptions and reliefs and reflected their desire to be viewed as rightful rulers of Egypt; they therefore downplayed their Nubian-ness.[38] The texts were modelled after Egyptian religious inscriptions: Pyramid Texts, Coffin Texts and the Book of the Dead. Variations in the texts do occur and are probably due to simple mistakes by the artisans working from a bad copy of the original text. The decorative programme also models an Egyptian format with representations of the Egyptian goddesses Nephthys at the head end and Isis at the foot of the sarcophagi, images of the Day and Night barques of the sun god accompanied by hymns to the rising and setting suns, and representations of the Four Sons of Horus, Imsety, Duamutef, Hapy and Qebehsenuef, who were responsible for guarding the organs removed during the mummification process.

Tanwetamani (c. 664–656 BC) and his mother, Queen Qalhata, decorated their tomb walls with Egyptian hieroglyphic inscriptions and combined Egyptian and Nubian imagery.[39] The king is shown in traditional Nubian fashion with a cloak knotted at the shoulder, an Amun-head pendant around his neck and the Kushite skullcap surmounted with a diadem with the double uraei at his brow, with streamers hanging down the back. The goddesses Isis and Nephthys are shown on the side of his chapel door along with two of the Four Sons of Horus: Duamutef and Qebehsenuef. Inside his burial chamber the walls are covered with scenes of Egyptian deities, the king as a ba-bird, a motif that becomes more prevalent during the Meroitic period, a solar barque carrying the sun disc with baboons and jackals worshipping it, and the Four Sons of Horus. There are also vertical columns and horizontal lines of hieroglyphs intertwined with these scenes.

His mother's tomb, located to the southwest of the kings' tombs, has a similar Egypto-Nubian decorative programme. The queen is shown wearing a broad-sleeved dress, a broad collar necklace and the vulture headdress of Egyptian queens atop the traditional Nubian close-cropped hairstyle. She is joined by the Four Sons of Horus. She is also shown mummified, lying on a bed with lions' heads. There is a scene of a man holding an ankh to the nose of her mummy, thereby ritually revivifying her. Similar to her son's decorations, she has a solar barque with baboons and jackals worshipping the sun disc and rows of Egyptian deities.

Pyramids continued to be constructed during the Meroitic period and could range in size. At the provincial site of Sedeinga, located about 725 kilometres (450 mi.) north of Meroe between the Second and Third Cataracts, pyramids were constructed for the Meroitic elite living in Lower Nubia. Hundreds of pyramids have been discovered ranging in width from 76.2 centimetres (30 in.) to 6.7 metres (22 ft). The smallest ones marked the graves of children.[40] The vast numbers and ranges of sizes of these pyramids could be because the site was so far removed from the capital that the inhabitants felt comfortable mimicking their southern rulers at a time when pyramids were still largely reserved for the royal family.

Offering tables were an integral part of elite and royal funerary religion at Meroe. They were generally square with a central basin or channel that surrounded an image. Inscriptions, written in either Egyptian hieroglyphs or the Meroitic cursive script, around the edge of the offering table were typically prayer formulae including the name of the deceased. A channel was carved from the 'spout' of the offering table so the libations could flow into the central basin. The tables were placed outside on the eastern side of the tomb entrance on top of a brick platform with funerary stelae and *ba*-statues near them.[41] The placement of the tables on platforms may have been so the priests could stand on the platforms while pouring the libations.

The image most frequently depicted on the offering tables was of deities pouring libations for the deceased. Anubis is usually shown giving the traditional offerings of water, wine, milk and meat along with the goddess Nephthys, who was possibly the mother of Anubis by Ra, Osiris or Seth. Other goddesses represented on offering tables include Isis, Ma'at, Meret and Nut. Anubis was sometimes shown with an unadorned female companion who might be a queen since they served as priestesses in Napatan and Meroitic religion.[42]

In Egyptian mythology Anubis was the patron deity of embalmers, and he aided the deceased on their journey to the afterlife during the weighing of the heart ceremony. He was typically depicted as a jackal-headed man or as a recumbent jackal lying atop a shrine. Anubis assumed a primary role in Meroitic funerary culture and was depicted on offering tables and door jambs. He was worshipped throughout the entirety of Meroitic history in his newfound mortuary context. Since embalming was not a common practice in Nubia, Anubis's role as the god of embalming evolved into him becoming a god of mortuary offerings. Graves from all social strata in Nubia contain mortuary offerings such as cups and jars that would be used by the deceased in the afterlife, which emphasized their recognition that food offerings were necessary to sustain them in the afterlife.

During the Meroitic period a cult of Dionysus emerged owing to continued interactions with the Mediterranean world. In Graeco-Roman Egypt Dionysus became associated with Osiris and eventually enhanced the Osirian myth of resurrection already established in Nubia.[43] The act of drinking wine and libations was connected with several important events including the New Year festival, the inundation and funerary feasts.[44] Wine became more prevalent as an accepted libation with the development of a Dionysian cult. Wine presses have been found at Lower Nubian sites, suggesting local wine production. Representations of Dionysus and the vine motif, associated with the god and resurrection, became more prevalent in decorations at this time.

Pottery with imagery of funerary feasts showing men dancing with palm branches, a water jar and a wine amphora have been found at Meroe.[45] A vessel from the later Meroitic-period cemeteries at Karanog has a depiction of satyrs performing a Dionysiac dance around amphorae. Scenes of Dionysus and the Dionysian cult are represented in the decorative programme of the palace of Natakamani and Amanitore at Jebel Barkal (B1500) and on the pottery found within. Vine and grape motifs are also present on the chapel walls of the pyramid of Queen Amanitore at Meroe and on an offering table from Wad ban Naga,[46] highlighting widespread acceptance of a Dionysian cult during the Meroitic period. The popularity of this cult continued into the Post-Meroitic period, particularly at Lower Nubian sites where contact between Graeco-Roman Egypt and Nubia would have been greater.

Religious practices and the depictions of their deities highlight how adaptable the Nubians were throughout their history. Along with the Egyptian, and eventual Ptolemaic, influences, the Nubians never lost sight of their roots and were able to incorporate representations of their own deities into temple scenes and adapt their traditions to suit their needs.

SIX

MEROE AND THE *KANDAKES*

As with many aspects of Nubian history, most of what we know about these remarkable women comes from the elite and royal realms. The Meroitic *kandakes* are some of the best-attested representations of powerful Nubian women, but they are certainly not the first women to play significant roles in the religious and political spheres of Nubia.

As far back as the Middle Kingdom, Nubian princesses were possibly marrying Egyptian princes. It has been suggested that two of the wives of Mentuhotep II, Ashayet and Kemsit, were of Nubian origin since their skin is painted black or with the reddish-brown hue traditional of Egyptian men, rather than the yellowish colour of Egyptian women. However, it is difficult to track the marriages since many of the women changed their names from their Nubian ones to Egyptian ones. Non-royal Nubian women most likely married Egyptian men as well, especially when they were living side by side while the Egyptian soldiers occupied the Second Cataract forts.

Women also served as priestesses. In Nubia the cult of Hathor, a cow-headed woman, may have easily been integrated into the local mindset given the high regard for cattle in Nubian society. During religious rites the Nubian priestesses would have performed indigenous dances, which were recorded by Egyptian artists.[1] During the New Kingdom, Egyptian queens and royal women held important offices that played a role in facilitating the rise of powerful Nubian women in Egypt.

Egyptian ruling queens

There is no official word in Egyptian for 'queen' and these powerful women were referred to by their relationship to the king or heir apparent: 'wife of the king', 'mother of the king', 'sister of the king' and 'daughter of the king'. Egyptian queens served as regents and participated in state politics.

Evidence for ruling queens in Egypt is sparse but did occasionally occur. A queen named Sobekneferu (*c.* 1777–1773 BC) possibly ruled at the end of Dynasty 12. Her name is listed in the Turin Canon but is omitted from the Abydos kings' list, which frequently deletes rulers deemed unworthy by Seti I (*c.* 1294–1279 BC) and his son Ramesses II. One of her statues shows her in female attire along with the *nemes* headdress of a king.

One of the most famous Egyptian ruling queens was Hatshepsut (*c.* 1473–1458 BC) from Dynasty 18 of the New Kingdom. She served as regent for the young Thutmose III and eventually claimed that she was the rightful heir to the Egyptian throne. Hatshepsut was the sole child of Thutmose I and his Great Royal Wife, Ahmose. She also fashioned herself as the divine daughter of the god Amun, an association used to legitimize her ascension to the throne. She commissioned several building projects during her reign, including the eighth pylon at Karnak, several obelisks and her mortuary temple at Deir el-Bahri, and conducted long-distance trade with Punt, which she documented on the walls of her mortuary temple. Ultimately, and obviously, Hatshepsut's reign was considered problematic by her successors. Thutmose III undertook a massive campaign during his reign to remove her name from the historical record. He also had her statues at Deir el-Bahri removed, destroyed and buried. Even his son, Amenhotep II, erased her name and images from her pylon at Karnak and recarved them for himself.

The last known ruling Egyptian queen was Tausret (*c.* 1188–1186 BC) at the end of Dynasty 19 of the New Kingdom. She originally served as regent for her husband's successor, Siptah, the son of a Syrian woman. Following Siptah's death, Tausret reigned as the sole ruling queen until her death.

God's wife of Amun

A new role for Egyptian women emerged in the New Kingdom (*c.* 1550–1070 BC) with the establishment of the title 'God's Wife of Amun' for Ahmose-Nefertari, the Great Royal Wife of Ahmose, the founder of Dynasty 18. This new office fell out of use after the reign of Hatshepsut in mid-Dynasty 18, yet would re-emerge in Dynasty 19 and continue to be used into the Third Intermediate Period (*c.* 1070–656 BC) in order for the ruling families to ensure the power base stayed within the family and could not be challenged. The women who held this office were granted privileges typically reserved for the king, such as being represented as a sphinx, being nursed by a goddess and receiving life from Amun.[2]

When the Nubian kings conquered Egypt and established Dynasty 25 (*c.* 760–656 BC), they maintained the practice and installed many of their daughters and sisters to the office. Kashta was the first king who installed his daughter, Amenirdis I, as God's Wife of Amun, thereby establishing himself as a protector of the Amun cult. She apparently ingratiated herself with the Theban elite because when Piye made his second campaign to Egypt, he was able to travel easily and safely through the Theban region.[3] Amenirdis I affirmed her legitimacy by constructing an addition to the chapel built by her predecessor Shepenwepet I, daughter of Osorkon III (*c.* 787–759 BC), showing the two of them making offerings to and receiving offerings from Amun, Mut and Isis. Amenirdis I was succeeded by her niece Shepenwepet II, Piye's daughter, who also worked to legitimize her new role. She built a new stone chapel at Medinet Habu that was adorned with reliefs showing her performing funerary rites for her aunt.[4] Shepenwepet II was succeeded by the daughter of Taharqo, Amenirdis II, who was the last Nubian princess to hold the office. It is worth noting that, as with the Nubian women who married Egyptian men, the God's Wives forewent their Nubian names and adopted Egyptian ones.

The passage of power from one God's Wife to another occurred through adoption, which ensured that the entire estate of the current God's Wife would fully transfer to her successor. When a change of rulership occurred, such as the establishment of Dynasties 25 and 26, the current God's Wife would be forced to adopt the new ruler's daughter or sister as her heir apparent, thus ensuring that the new ruling family would gain control over this powerful office and by extension the Theban region. The adoption process was documented on the Nitocris Adoption Stela and the Ankhnesneferibre Adoption Stela from Dynasty 26 on which the transfer of property and the installation ceremonies were described.

It is particularly interesting that the God's Wives highlighted their femininity along with their power.[5] One point of debate among scholars is the issue of celibacy. It remains uncertain whether or not these women were permitted to marry; however, their long lifespans do suggest that they did not bear children. Furthermore, given the level of power and influence these women possessed, it is possible that the king wanted to prevent them from creating their own dynasties, which would have threatened his power.[6]

Early Nubian queens

The Kerma period (*c.* 2500–1450 BC) saw the rise of a powerful Nubian kingdom, yet their lack of written language prevents us from knowing the names of their kings and queens. One possible burial of a Kerman queen comes from a subsidiary burial K1053 in Tumulus KX dated to the Kerma Classique.[7] The woman was buried in the traditional Kerman style on an inlaid funerary bed surrounded by lavish imported and local grave goods. Her body was adorned with jewellery, and she wore a silver headdress and a leather skirt with silver beading on the drawstring.[8] Her attire and grave goods place the woman buried in K1053 alongside high-status Kerman females, possibly priestesses or members of the royal family.

Prior to the rise of the Napatan (*c.* 800–300 BC) kings was a woman named Katimalo or Karimalo, who bore the titles 'king's great wife' and 'king's daughter' on an inscription. She is an obscure figure during this early period of Nubian history. Her inscription was written on the southern facade of the Temple of Dedwen and Senwosret III at Semna and it remains the only evidence of her to date. The text is accompanied by a scene to the left of the main inscription that shows a woman facing left wearing the tight sheath dress typical of Egyptian women and goddesses, a broad collar and a cow's horn headdress. The inscription names her as the goddess Isis. In her right hand she holds a bouquet and in her left an *ankh*. A second woman, facing the first, is shown wearing a loose cloak on top of a tight sheath dress. This attire is reminiscent of late New Kingdom Ramesside queens or may be a precursor to the Nubian cloak worn by Napatan queens. Her jewellery is simple: a broad collar, a pair of earrings, and two armbands on her upper arms. She is adorned with a vulture headdress, typical of Egyptian queens, which is surmounted with the tall plumes and sun disc of the god Amun along with streamers hanging down the back. She does not wear the long, elaborate wig of an Egyptian queen but rather the short, curly hairstyle of Nubian women. Above her is the flying vulture of the goddess Nekhbet, who protects the queen. In her left hand she is holding the flail of Egyptian kingship and in her right what may be a dagger. In front of her is an inscription in which she styles herself as the 'great King's Wife of the King of Upper and Lower Egypt and king's daughter.' The small female figure behind Katimalo also wears the short Nubian hairstyle along with the Egyptian sheath dress. She holds a mirror in her right hand and a piece of fabric, possibly a scarf, in her left. It is possible that she is a princess.[9] The text opens with the date of regnal year 14, month two of winter, day nine of an unnamed king who refers to himself as 'majesty' and 'pharaoh'.[10] He describes enemy attacks and pleads to Katimalo for help. The regular use of the term 'justified' at the end of her name indicates this text was inscribed after she was already deceased. The king's plea to her could be an attempt to call upon her magic to ensure his victory. This is similar to the Egyptian tradition of writing letters to the dead to ask them for help.

Based on the Late Egyptian grammatical constructions and the inclusion of some elements of Demotic and Coptic, this text can be dated to the so-called 'dark age' of Nubian history that occurred during the Egyptian Third Intermediate Period (Dynasties 21–24/25).[11] It has been suggested that she might have been the wife of the Dynasty 21 Egyptian king, Siamun (*c.* 978–959 BC).[12]

However, this would place her significantly earlier than her Napatan successors of the second half of the eighth century BC. Her name, from the Meroitic meaning 'good lady', indicates a southern, Meroitic origin for her, which would align with the northward journey of the southern Nubians to join forces with Kashta (*c.* 760–747 BC) and his army for his Egyptian campaign.[13] Her titles indicate that she was of royal lineage, but it is uncertain whether her family ties were to the kings of Kush, who later fashioned themselves as king of Upper and Lower Egypt, or a king of Lower Nubia.[14] For these reasons, it is more probable that she was a daughter and queen of a Nubian ruler, not the wife of an Egyptian king.

Napatan queens in the coronation ceremonies

Royal women in Nubia, particularly the king's mother and sister(s), were an integral element to the king's legitimization. In Napatan society the role of the king's mother was defined by her relationship with her son, much like the role of Isis to her son Horus. The king's mother and wife were always shown in Napatan coronation scenes. Conversely, it was the king's responsibility to venerate his female lineage, and the kings frequently lauded their mothers and sisters on their stelae. To be a legitimate king, he needed to be the son of a king's sister. In order to further enhance his claim to the throne, whenever possible, the king traced his female lineage to Pebatma, the sister of Alara, who founded the Napatan dynasty. This connection with the female line has caused some scholars to support a system of matrilineal succession in Nubia, although this cannot be proven or refuted with current evidence.

The importance of the king's mother during the coronation ceremonies is attested through her role as a sistrum shaker. Royal women were also responsible for pouring libations, such as water or milk, before Amun. Offering libations to the god was a privilege traditionally associated in Egypt with the king, making the female appropriation of this function in Nubian iconography notable. Royal women are first shown performing this rite during Dynasty 25, probably when they took over the act.

The lunettes of the enthronement stelae include scenes of the kings' coronations with female family members in attendance, shaking a sistrum or pouring libations. Their presence and participation at the coronation ceremonies were neither ornamental nor accidental. The importance of the king's mother in his coronation ceremonies was a Nubian adaptation of the Egyptian mythology surrounding Isis and Horus. Egyptian royal legitimization was not reliant on the king's mother's participation in his coronation ceremonies.

Since Aspelta was too young to ascend the throne, his mother, Queen Nasalsa, became his regent. A stela of Aspelta dedicated to Prince Khaliut, a deceased son of Piye and relative of Aspelta, mentions that the king and his mother are together as he sits on the throne, 'appearing as King-of-Upper-and-Lower-Egypt on the throne of Horus of the living forever, together with the king's mother Nasalsa, may she live, as Isis did with her son Horus in Two-lands'.[15] On the Election Stela of Aspelta, his mother, Nasalsa, is shown shaking two sistra in front of Amun, Mut and her son. Interestingly, the face and cartouches of his mother were erased along with the cartouches of his female lineage. This could indicate that his matrilineal line was rejected by a faction that wanted to replace him with another ruler.[16]

Aspelta Enthronement Stela from the Amun Temple at Jebel Barkal.

The king's mother also travelled with him on the coronation journey and made speeches to Amun asking him to bestow the kingship upon him. Taharqo's mother journeyed to Memphis for his coronation while the mothers of Anlamani and Irike-Amannote journeyed to Napata.

Following the coronation ceremonies, the kings' mothers could celebrate the successful ascension of their sons. Taharqo and Anlamani both describe how their mothers were joyful upon seeing them on the throne:

> She (Taharqo's mother Abar) found me appearing on the throne of Horus (in Memphis), after I had received the diadems of Re, and was wearing the uraei on my head . . . She was exceedingly joyful after seeing the beauty of His Majesty, (just) as Isis saw her son Horus appearing on the throne of his father Osiris.[17]
>
> (When) she (Anlamani's mother Nasalsa) found her son effulgent (that is, radiant) like Horus on his throne, and she was exceedingly joyful after she saw His Majesty's beauty, (just) as Isis (was when she) saw her son Horus effulgent on earth.[18]

The only known potentially ruling queen from the Napatan period is Sakhmakh, the widow of Nastaseñ (last third of the fourth century BC). She was styled as 'king' on her stela from Jebel Barkal, but the remainder of the inscription is not legible, so it is uncertain what is meant by her possibly holding the title of 'king'.

Dynasty 25 and Napatan royal women were buried in the royal cemeteries at el-Kurru and Nuri. The tombs at el-Kurru dedicated to these women were located to the north and south of the kings' tombs. Scant inscriptional evidence remains, leaving the roles and status of these women unclear. The tombs of royal women buried at Nuri can be found in the western portion of the cemetery. Based on the surviving inscriptions, the kings' mothers were given the largest tombs.

Powerful women in political positions is in evidence in contemporary Assyrian contexts as well. Sammuramat, the mother of

Adad-Nirari III (*c.* 811–783 BC), and Naqia-Zakûtu, the mother of Esarhaddon (*c.* 681–669 BC), were not only politically active but able to influence the court to allow their sons to become kings, even though they were not the heirs to the throne.[19]

Meroitic *kandakes*

The first century BC and first century AD of the Meroitic period gave rise to strong, powerful queens called *kandakes*. This title was reserved for the king's sister and mother of the future king, thus continuing the importance of the female line in Meroitic society. Three queens also held the title *qore*, which was typically reserved for the king and so suggests that they were sole-ruling queens. These sole-ruling and, at times, warrior queens were depicted

Queen Amanitore smiting enemies, from the Lion Temple at Naqa.

alongside their husbands on temple pylons smiting enemies. The queens also assumed more traditional kingly duties, including leading rituals previously performed by the king.

Textual accounts of the queens of Meroe come primarily from Classical sources. In a story set during the reign of Alexander the Great, it is said that Alexander exchanged letters with the queen of Meroe and visited her in Nubia. He was enthralled by the idea of meeting her:

> He earnestly desired to see it, for it was very famous in the whole country and in Greece . . . A woman ruled over the city, she was extremely beautiful, in the prime of life, and [a descendant] of Queen Semiramis. To her Alexander sent a letter with the follow contents: 'King Alexander greets Queen Candace of Meroe and the rulers subject to her' . . . On his way (to Meroe) Alexander marvelled at the many-coloured mountains of rock-crystal, reaching up to the clouds in the sky, and at the trees with their lofty foliage, laden with fruit. They were not like those of the Greeks, but wonders of their own.[20]

Whether or not Alexander actually visited Meroe is uncertain, but it does show that the use of the title was known to foreign rulers. However, the title eventually evolved and became the modern-day personal name Candice.

The importance of this title was also known to Greek and Roman visitors to Nubia such as Bion of Soloi, a third century BC writer, who mentioned that '*Candace* is what the Aithiopians (Nubians) call every mother of a king . . . "The Aithiopians do not reveal who are the fathers of their kings, but these are traditionally regarded as sons of the sun (probably Amun)."'[21]

The first known Meroitic queen to ascend to the throne was Queen Shanadakheto (first half of first century BC).[22] She was not titled *qore*, which usually suggested a ruling queen, but she was buried in the Northern Cemetery where the rulers of Meroe were buried. In the funerary chapel of her pyramid, she was shown with a prince holding the streamers hanging down from her headdress, as was performed during the coronation ceremonies.

The next ruling queen, Nawidemak, followed three male rulers.[23] She did fashion herself as *qore* instead of *kandake*. Little is known about her reign and we do not know why she chose not to be buried at Meroe. Instead, she opted to construct her pyramid and be buried at Napata (Jebel Barkal), as did her two predecessors.

Queen Amanirenas (last third of the first century BC) held the title of *kandake* and *qore*, indicating she was a ruling queen. She was probably the wife of King Teriteqas, since she appears as a non-ruling queen on his stela from Meroe. In 25 BC the Nubian army, under the leadership of a 'one-eyed *kandake*', raided and looted the Roman-controlled towns of Philae, Syene and Elephantine, located in the First Cataract region. This one-eyed queen, who fought C. Petronius in the war between Meroe and Rome mentioned by Strabo, is thought to be Amanirenas. This conflict has presumably been documented on the Meroitic stelae of Amanirenas and Prince Akinidad found at Hamadab, based on the words *Arme* and *Qes*, 'Rome and Kush'.[24] One of the most famous spoils of these raids is the bronze head of Augustus that was ritually buried upside down beneath the stairs leading into Temple M292 at Meroe. This would have allowed anyone entering and exiting the temple to trample over the Roman ruler's head. Amanirenas was also buried at Napata instead of at Meroe.

Queen Amanishakheto ruled during the end of the first century BC and the beginning of the first century AD. She may have been another wife of King Teriteqas and ultimately succeeded Amanirenas since, for unknown reasons, Akinidad never became the ruler despite being identified as the crown prince '*pqr*' and heir apparent.[25] Amanishakheto constructed a large 61-metre (200 ft) mudbrick palace at Wad ban Naga. Its 45 rooms are primarily rectilinear in shape and most were storerooms. The building has been attributed to the reign of Queen Amanishakheto because of a cartouche bearing her name discovered within the palace.

The main entrance was located on the southern side of the building and a central door led to a hypostyle hall with six sandstone columns. To the left and right of the hypostyle hall are

Opposite: Bronze head of Augustus.

four doors that lead to storerooms containing pottery, a small altar, sandstone lions and terracotta hawks. A second door at the northern end of the hypostyle hall led to an anteroom. Originally there were five entrances on the ground level: three were service entrances, and the other two may have been grand entrances. On the eastern side of the building a ramp stretched approximately 21 metres (69 ft) along the outside of the building. This ramp provided access to the second storey of the building.

Even though the upper storey of the palace is no longer preserved, some of its characteristics can be discerned from elements found on the lower level. The original placement of sandstone columns from the second floor is suggested by load-bearing columns found on the lower level. The walls of the upper levels would have been highly decorated with faience and stone ornaments of animal and vegetal motifs as well as images of the queen.[26]

Although this palace is the best-preserved royal residence from the Meroitic period, only the ground floor of the plan can be reliably reconstructed. Of all the rooms and corridors present, up to sixty in total, only five rooms can confidently be labelled as storerooms.[27] Inside one of the storerooms the excavators discovered a deposit of elephant tusks and wooden planks, which might have provided the royal workshops with raw materials for ivory and ebony. In the middle of the layer was found a shiny spherical black vase. Similar objects were found in some of the other storerooms and they appeared in relatively large quantities.

Nubia had long been known for its golden riches. The nineteenth-century Italian physician Giuseppe Ferlini, serving as surgeon major in the Egyptian army, requested permission to 'excavate' sites north of Khartoum in search of these treasures.[28] He partnered with Antonio Stefani, an Albanian merchant in Khartoum, and they travelled to Meroe in 1834 following unsuccessful excursions to Naqa and Wad ban Naga. Seeing the pyramid fields at Meroe, he focused on uncovering their secrets. After opening a series of tombs that were devoid of gold and jewels, he began 'excavating' one of the largest tombs in the Northern Cemetery, Begarawiya North 6 (Beg. N. 6), the tomb of Queen Amanishakheto. Ferlini and his team dismantled the pyramid

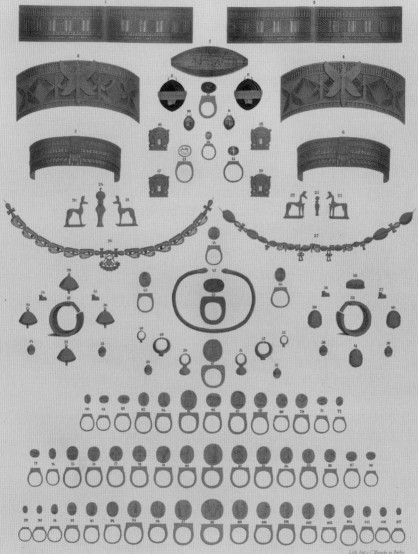

Begerauieh Pyramidengruppe A. Pyr. 15.
Gold- und Silber-Schmuck aufgefunden von Ferlini 1830. (jetzt im K. Mus. zu Berlin.)

Jewellery of Amanishakheto.

stone by stone to the level of the chapel. They were left disappointed but not discouraged. He subsequently dismissed the workmen and began digging around the chapel in secret until, behind a wall, he found the burial chamber, which contained one of the finest collections of Nubian jewellery ever unearthed. Following his return to Europe, Ferlini sold part of the collection to King Ludwig I of Bavaria (this was later presented to the Staatliche Sammlung für Ägyptische Kunst in Munich) and the remainder was acquired by the Ägyptisches Museum in Berlin.

Amanitore reigned alongside her husband, Natakamani, during the mid-first century AD. Their reign was marked by an extensive building programme in which temples were built or rebuilt throughout the country. Palace decoration now adhered to the new fashion of incorporating Mediterranean iconography. Most notably, Meroitic replaced Egyptian as the language of choice for monumental inscriptions.[29]

Artistic representations

Representations of women in Egyptian art differ from depictions of Nubian women. Egyptian women and anthropoid goddesses were shown as petite, lithe figures in tight sheath dresses. Royal women were frequently shown wearing the vulture headdress, thus connecting the queen or princess with the goddess Nekhbet or Mut. In the New Kingdom, royal women also adopted head-dresses embellished with cow horns and a sun disc to link them with Hathor. The God's Wives of Amun in Thebes followed similar imagery as the Egyptian queens, wearing a sheath dress and long-haired wigs. They were frequently shown wearing the vulture headdress surmounted by the tall plumes of Amun and a sun disc.

The Napatan queens incorporated Nubian stylistic elements into their representations. They are shown wearing a long, flowing cloak, which could be draped over either one shoulder or both and could be decorated with a fringe. The cloak was typically worn over a shorter dress and was tied at the shoulders. An animal tail, possibly that of a fox, hung down the back.[30] Instead of wearing the long wigs of Egyptian queens, they sported the tight, curly hairstyles of Nubian women. They also did not frequently wear the vulture headdress, as seen on Egyptian queens, but rather opted for a diadem with a lotus or *uraeus* serpent at the brow. They could also be shown wearing a headdress of cow horns with a sun disc and tall feathers.

In contrast to the delicate representations of Egyptian and Napatan queens, the Meroitic *kandakes* and *qores* were shown as much more robust. They have prominent hips, thighs and large breasts, emphasizing their powerful positions. They are shown wearing attire similar to that of their husbands, with a pleated and fringed cloak atop a long undergarment. A tasselled cord hangs from their shoulders. The queens could also be depicted wearing a feathered dress and they were often adorned with heavy jewellery and sandals.

The legacy of the *kandakes* continues to resonate today. Women of all ages and backgrounds played an important role during the 2018–19 pro-democracy protests in Sudan, making up about 70 per cent of the demonstrators. They voiced their frustrations about the country's sexism and the harsh practices of Sharia law. One woman, Alaa Salah, a 22-year-old engineering and architecture student at Sudan International University, was dubbed 'Kandaka' after the Meroitic word for queen, *kandake*.[31] In a photograph that went viral, she wears a taub or tobe, the traditional attire of Sudanese women, yet unlike the popular colourful variations, hers is white. Wearing a white taub became a symbol for female activists and Salah herself became an important symbol of the protests, reminding the demonstrators of Sudan's history of powerful women.

SEVEN
MOVING INTO THE
IRON AGE

The Napatan and Meroitic economies relied heavily on commerce. Since agriculture was not on the scale seen in Egypt, cities the size of Napata or Meroe would still have required enough agricultural surplus to feed the considerable non-agricultural population, which included ironworkers, masons, potters and other craftsmen. Food surpluses could also have been used to employ labour for building projects such as temples, tombs and palaces, but the required surpluses may not have been able to be stored for long periods of time. Therefore the Nubian economy might not have been centralized as it was in Egypt. Instead the Meroitic state, and presumably the Napatan state as well, may have consisted of small subsistence farmers who did not contribute to the state and, subsequently, did not receive anything from the state to supplement their crops.

Through established trade relations, the royal and noble tombs at Meroe had an abundance of wealth placed within them, whereas the non-elite tombs were quite poor. However, a different situation was occurring in the northern provinces, particularly at Qasr Ibrim, which is located north of Faras between the First and Second Cataracts in present-day southern Egypt.

A large weaving industry at Qasr Ibrim developed sometime in the early first century AD when the inhabitants were introduced to cotton by Meroitic people arriving from the south.[1] The people of Qasr Ibrim began producing cotton items that were retained locally as well as traded to Egypt. Although the oldest cotton fragments – from Ballana, Qustul, Jebel Adda and Qasr Ibrim – have been dated to the Roman period around the first century AD, the majority of the cotton remains coincide with the height of the later Meroitic civilization in Lower Nubia, dating to around AD 200–330.[2] After the collapse of this empire, a shift occurred from the use of cotton to wool, primarily camels' wool, for the production of textiles. In the Post-Meroitic period (*c.* AD 350–550), woollen textiles accounted for 93 per cent of textiles from Ballana and Qustul, and 90 per cent from Jebel Adda. The shift from cotton to wool may have taken place due to a change in population or culture after the fall of Meroe and, subsequently, resulted in the decline of the Lower Nubian economy, since their primary source of wealth depended upon the export of cotton fabrics.

The premise that cotton may have been grown in the region of Meroe and transported to Lower Nubia for production purposes is based on a stela of King Ezana (*c.* AD 330–70) discovered at Aksum, which describes his war against the Noba and the subsequent destruction of Meroe. Ezana states that he and his men 'destroyed the statues of their houses (that is, temples), and the treasuries of food, and the cotton trees, and cast them into the River Sêdâ (Nile)'.[3] Additionally, Upper Nubia is located in the rain belt, which would have provided an environment conducive to the growth of cotton. The use of the *saqia* waterwheel may have allowed Lower Nubians to irrigate their lands and grow cotton in the region between Derr and Toshka at Aniba, located opposite Qasr Ibrim.[4] It is unfortunate that the lack of additional archaeological evidence, along with needing the precise identification of the source of cotton used at Qasr Ibrim, prevents us from knowing exactly how the Nubian cotton industry operated.

The presence of a thriving centre of production in Lower Nubia may be the reason that a greater amount of luxury goods have been found in the cemeteries there.[5] Trade relations between Lower Nubia and Ptolemaic Egypt intensified during the reign of Arqamani (*c.* 248–220 BC) and it appears that, after contact with Ptolemaic Egypt, Lower Nubia became an economic and commercial extension of the Roman Empire, yet remained politically subservient to the Meroitic crown.[6]

Nubian metalworking

Early metalworking focused on the manipulation of copper for weapons, tools and jewellery. Copper was used widely throughout Predynastic Egypt (c. 5300–3000 BC), and items were traded south to Nubia towards the end of the period. Copper working was also developing in western Africa in the first millennium BC.

Being a softer metal, copper could be easily shaped and decorated in a variety of ways. Despite the metal's softness being beneficial for alteration, copper tools had to be regularly reshaped in order to remain fit for use. Therefore a new, harder metal needed to be found to suit their needs. When it was discovered that combining copper with tin created alloyed bronze, this new material was used to make sturdier tools and weapons.

Metals became popular trade commodities and could be exchanged for raw materials from other groups. During the New Kingdom, Egypt began trading bronze items throughout the Mediterranean and along the northern coast of Africa.

The transition from the Bronze Age to the Iron Age in sub-Saharan Africa occurred prior to the Meroitic period in Nubia. Ironworking techniques had already been developed in Anatolia by the Hittites around 1500 BC and imported iron objects can be found in Egypt around 1000 BC. The iron weapons used by the Assyrians were superior to the bronze weapons used by the Egyptians, possibly contributing to Egypt's defeat.

Ironworking at Meroe

The capital at Meroe shows evidence of a substantial ironworking industry that might be one of the earliest in the region. Remains of slag, furnaces, charcoal and ore have been found just outside the modern entrance to the Royal City. Early archaeologists commented on the prevalence of ironworking remains at Meroe:

> Mountains of iron-slag enclose the city-mounds on their northern and eastern sides, and excavation has brought to light the furnaces in which the iron was smelted and fashioned

Iron slag at Meroe.

into tools and weapons. Meroë, in fact, must have been the Birmingham of ancient Africa; the smoke of its iron-smelting furnaces must have been continually going up to heaven, and the whole of northern Africa might have been supplied by it with implements of iron. Where the Egyptians used copper or bronze, the Ethiopians (that is, Nubians) used iron.[7]

One of the most taxing parts of smelting iron is the amount of wood needed to make charcoal for the fires, and as a result areas that were not heavily wooded, such as Egypt, had difficulties developing this technology. Meroe was an ideal location for the development of ironworking, since the hills east of the city had abundant iron ore deposits and the area was heavily wooded with acacia trees in ancient times. The earliest evidence for ironworking at the site dates to the Napatan period and continued for the next thousand years.[8]

Meroitic ironworkers used bloomery smelting technology, which occurs within a furnace and uses charcoal for its heat source.[9] Furnaces were dome-shaped structures built of burnt brick with six sets of bellows surrounding the furnace and two

holes allowing for the attachment of tuyères (nozzles for forcing air into the furnace). These types of furnaces were probably introduced to Nubia in the first century AD when the Meroites had contact with Rome. Prior to these furnaces, slag pits were probably used.[10] The furnace was then heated to 1,200°C (2,192°F). This process produces slag, which transports the iron particles and protects it from re-oxidizing.[11] A successful smelt yielded a spongy iron bloom that would then be refined through smithing. Ironworking provided employment for a large portion of the population: people were needed to collect the ore in the hills and make the charcoal, while specialized smelters managed the furnaces.

Large mounds of iron slag and debris have been found outside the Royal City. Based on the amount of slag remaining at Meroe, it has been estimated that approximately 5 to 20 tonnes of iron objects were produced each year for about five hundred years.[12] The development of ironworking allowed for production of better weapons, particularly arrowheads, which would have not only been instrumental in securing the borders but played into the increased warrior king ideology of the Meroitic period.

Recent archaeological excavations have also identified metalworking furnaces. Evidence for pre-Meroitic iron objects is scarce but iron foundation deposits were excavated at the pyramids of Nuri.[13] The majority of ironworking, however, occurred later in Nubian history.[14] Many of the objects found are utilitarian, however, and early iron objects are rarely found at Meroe, suggesting that many pieces, once deemed unusable, were melted down and recycled or suitable objects were exported. In the later Meroitic period, iron-tipped arrows and spears become common burial goods. Iron also played an important role in the Meroitic economy as it was exported along with gold, ivory, ostrich feathers and other exotic African products.

The location of ironworking areas near palaces and temples suggests a high degree of royal control. A temple dedicated to Apedemak was constructed atop a slag mound in the southeastern part of Meroe. We have already explored Apedemak's role in

Experimental ironworking furnace at Meroe.

the legitimization of the king, but the deity's warlike aspects may have also been connected with the king's military might through ironworking.[15]

The spread of ironworking to West Africa

The extensive quantities of iron ore throughout sub-Saharan Africa enabled ironworking to develop and spread at various sites. It is uncertain whether ironworking knowledge and technology first developed at Meroe and then spread into other areas of Africa or if West African sites developed the technology independently. Evidence for copper smelting can be found in Mauritania near Akjoujt and in Niger near Agadez during the fifth century BC.[16] An ironworking industry discovered at Taruga in Nigeria was contemporary with Meroitic ironworking.[17] Although there is evidence for early contact between West and North African cultures, there is no reason to believe that the spread of ironworking was dependent on these interactions. The wooded areas of West Africa provided the inhabitants with the necessary wood supplies to create charcoal and by 400 BC ironworking was thriving, which allowed for expanded agricultural practices and hunting.

The earliest evidence for West African ironworking comes from the Nok, who settled in the Niger region at the confluence of the Niger and Benue rivers around 1500 BC. They were specialized potters and created elaborate figurines. Nok settlements dating between the fifth and third centuries BC have remains of ironworking furnaces. It is unknown whether their proficiency with ceramics pre-dated their ironworking knowledge. The Nok disappeared around the early first millennium AD under unknown circumstances. Ironworking later spread throughout West Africa during the first millennium AD, culminating in the rise of the kingdom of Ghana.

Ironworking legacies

The Kuku peoples inhabit the city of Kajo-Kaji, located about 150 kilometres (93 mi.) south of Juba, in present-day South Sudan. Their language is part of the Eastern Nilotic branch of the Nilo-Saharan language family. They practised agriculture and pastoralism as early as AD 500. The Kuku peoples are believed to be descendants of the ancient Meroites.[18] They migrated from Meroe in several waves beginning in the early 1300s, travelling east into modern-day Eritrea, through southwestern Ethiopia, and eventually settling at Kajo-Kaji along the border between South Sudan and Uganda.

Prior to developing blacksmithing techniques, the Kuku used ironwood, a hardwood prevalent in sub-Saharan Africa. One of the most interesting cultural aspects of the Kuku is their blacksmithing tradition, which developed during the eighteenth century. As with ancient societies, Kuku blacksmiths primarily produced utilitarian wares such as agricultural implements, weapons, arrow- and spearheads, as well as knives and axes. Kuku elders believed that ironworking knowledge was passed down from the god Sagu, possibly a shadow of the connection between Meroitic ironworking and the god Apedemak.[19]

Sadly, the legacy of the Kuku blacksmiths has been lost due to the civil wars that ravaged South Sudan (1955–72, 1983–2005) and caused the displacement of many members of this ethnic group. All photographs were either destroyed or lost when many Kuku peoples fled to Uganda:

> It is very unfortunate that the institution of blacksmithing has disappeared in the Kuku society. I hope that when permanent peace comes to that war-torn country (South Sudan), the institution will be revived. At that time, I would encourage the descendants of blacksmiths to revive it as a vocation, similar to what their ancestors had done.[20]

EIGHT
FROM NUBIA TO
SUDAN

The end of the Meroitic period marked a return to independent polities governed by local rulers. During his
excavations in Nubia, George Reisner labelled the period
following the end of the Meroitic Empire as the 'X-Group', in keep-
ing with his previous classifications of earlier periods in Nubian
history as A-Group, 'B-Group' (later disproved) and C-Group. He
recognized that the materials discovered were culturally different
from the A-, 'B-' and C-Group remains, so he jumped to the end of
the alphabet to leave room for discoveries that would fall between
these early and late phases.

Post-Meroitic Nubia

Regional centres of power developed at Ballana and Qustul in
Lower Nubia, Tanqasi near Napata and el-Hobagi near Meroe.
Royal burials from the Post-Meroitic (c. AD 350–550) period were
identified at Ballana and Qustul, where the largest tomb measured
77 metres (263 ft) in diameter and 13 metres (43 ft) in height.[1] These
tomb superstructures reverted back to tumulus tombs, typically
only with a single burial. The bodies were buried on funerary beds
in the foetal position. As in the Kerma period, human and animal
sacrifices were included with royal burials. With the advent of
ironworking during the Meroitic period, iron weapons and tools
were among the traditional grave goods of pottery, bronze objects,
jewellery and cosmetic tools. Contact with Christian Egypt is evident through royal grave goods. A crown from a royal tomb at

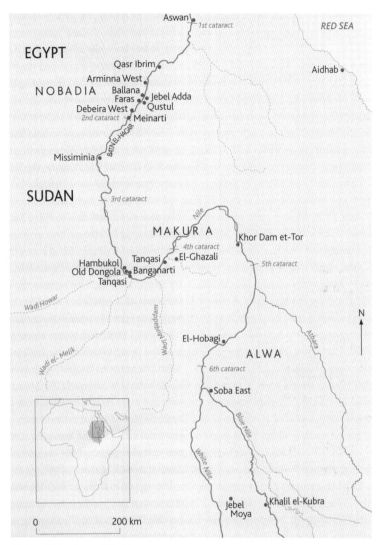

Medieval kingdoms of Nubia.

Ballana was Byzantine in style but incorporated indigenous iconography as well, such as Nubian deities, *uraeus* serpents and a ram's head. Despite the elaborate metalwork that could be found, pottery was simply decorated.

Power eventually began to consolidate at three centres throughout Nubia. Little is known about the rise of these smaller states, yet by the end of the fifth century the Lower Nubian site of

Nobadia (capital at Faras) began to develop, followed by the Upper Nubian sites of Makuria (capital at Old Dongola) and Alwa (capital at Soba East) in the sixth century. The rulers at Nobadia continued to represent themselves in the traditional Meroitic royal regalia and worshipped Nubian deities. However, by this time Meroitic was no longer the state language and had been replaced by Greek in the north. The last known Meroitic inscription was carved in the Temple of Mandulis at Kalabsha. It was of a local Lower Nubian ruler, Kharamadoye, dating to the late fourth or early fifth century and is one of the longest known Meroitic inscriptions.

King Silko, ruler of the Nobatai, conquered the Blemmyes in the mid-fifth century, recording the event in a Greek victory inscription on the Temple of Mandulis at Kalabsha. He describes his triumph over his enemies and the consolidation of his power:

> I, Silko, King (basiliskos) of the Noubades and all the Aithiopians, came to Talmis (Kalabsha) and Taphis (Tafa). On two occasions I fought with the Blemmyes; and God gave me the victory. On the third occasion I was again victorious and took control of their cities. I occupied (them) with my troops . . . When I had become king (basiliskos), I did not by any means proceed behind the other kings (basileus), but well ahead of them. For those who contend with me I do not permit to remain settled in their country unless they have beseeched me and entreat me. For I am a lion in the lower regions, and a bear in the upper regions.[2]

In the Post-Meroitic period a fort system was developed along the Nile in the Fourth Cataract region. This may have been due to the decentralization of the government and the rise of localized rulers in Upper Nubia. Classical writers had indicated that different ethnic groups may have controlled the area. Strabo wrote, 'As the Libyans occupy the western bank of the Nile, and the Ethiopians the country on the other side of the river, they dispute by turns the possession of the islands and the banks of the river, one party repulsing the other, or yielding to the superiority of its opponent,' whereas Ptolemy indicated that the Nubae controlled the area.[3]

Desert outposts associated with these forts would have allowed scouts to monitor the comings and goings of desert and riverine traffic, and identify desert incursions from nomadic groups.[4]

Christianization of Nubia

Christianity was introduced in the mid-sixth century and conversion was relatively rapid. By this time Egypt, the Mediterranean and southwest Asia had all been converted.[5] Conversion occurred separately throughout Nobadia, Makuria and Alwa. The initial motive to Christianize Nubia stemmed from the Byzantine Empire and the rivalry between the theologies promoted by the Dyophysites, who believed Christ had a divine and human nature, and the Monophysites, who believed Christ had only a divine nature.[6] Conversion occurred from north to south, starting with the Nobadian kingdom by the Monophysite missionaries sent by Empress Theodora of Constantinople. The date of the official conversion of the Makurian kingdom is unclear but appears to have followed shortly after that of Nobadia. Alodia was the final kingdom to convert. By 580 Christianity had spread throughout Nubia and become the official state religion.

By the eighth century Nobadia and Makuria were united and ruled by the king of Makuria, who resided in Old Dongola, and his deputy who initially governed from Faras and later from Qasr Ibrim, Jebel Adda and Meinarti.[7] Although combined under a single ruler, the formerly independent Nobadia and Makauria behaved differently. Egyptian merchants in Nobadia traded their goods and were permitted to settle in the area, and Egyptian coins were considered viable currency. Foreigners were not welcomed in Makuria, however, unless granted a royal dispensation, the barter system still prevailed, and the royal family controlled commerce.[8] Meanwhile Alodia remained independent and, despite some minor skirmishes, the two kingdoms seemingly lived in peace.

Egypt had converted to Islam by 641. The Arab army attacked Makuria but was driven away by Nubian archers. True to their reputation as famed archers, the invading Muslims called them 'eyesmiters' due to their accuracy. In 652 Christian Nubia and Muslim Egypt agreed terms for a peace treaty, known as the 'Baqt' (pact), which regulated trade between the countries for almost six hundred years. Under this treaty, Aswan and Qasr Ibrim became centres of trade. Gold, ivory and slaves from Nubia were exchanged for Egyptian textiles, ceramics and glass.

The Christian period was markedly different from those that preceded it and emphasized the speed of conversion. Christian-period tombs were generally simple, only containing the body of the deceased wrapped in a shroud or placed in a coffin. They were typically oriented east–west and interspersed with tombs from earlier periods. Conversely, the tombs of the clergy sometimes had inscriptions on the walls.[9]

Unlike previous periods, grave goods were no longer included in tombs. When available, funerary inscriptions lack references to family members, possibly indicating that familial ties were less important than in earlier periods. However, Christian Nubians appear to have been concerned with legal systems, as evidenced by the sheer number of legal documents uncovered from Qasr Ibrim.

At this time some Egyptian and Nubian temples were converted into churches alongside the construction of new churches and monasteries. These churches shared similarities with churches from the Byzantine Empire, Syro-Palestine, Coptic Egypt and Ethiopia. True to Nubian customs, however, they combined features from different cultures and added indigenous features, culminating in a uniquely Nubian-style church.[10] Nubian churches were frequently constructed using both mud-brick and stone, unlike ancient temples that were built solely out of stone. In Nubia church services were conducted in Greek and not Coptic, as in Egypt.

In the eighth century churches began to be decorated with elaborate paintings. Many of these murals have been lost except at the site of Faras, which dates from the seventh to fourteenth centuries AD. Excavation of this site was conducted during the 1960s under the UNESCO Nubian Salvage campaign prior to the area being flooded by Lake Nasser. During excavations a total of 169 paintings were discovered.[11] They were executed in tempera on dry plaster. Additionally, approximately 750 inscriptions, including a

Pilgrim flask with horned serpents from Meinarti, dating to the medieval Christian period.

list documenting the names and tenures of the Bishops of Faras, were recorded in Greek, Coptic and Old Nubian. The paintings consisted of Christian themes such as the Madonna and Child, Apostles, Christ, Archangels, and St George and the dragon.

Christian-period pottery initially continued the simplicity of Post-Meroitic pottery but eventually returned to the Meroitic traditions of detailed decoration. Images included geometric designs, vegetal motifs, animals such as birds, fish and serpents, and *ankh*-style crosses. Religious texts, which mostly consisted of traditional church liturgy, were written in Old Nubian, Coptic, Greek or a combination of these languages.[12] The prevalence of written documents indicates a high rate of literacy, which starkly contrasts with earlier periods.

Saladin overthrew the Fatimid rulers in Egypt in 1172 and proceeded to attack northern Nubia, though without success. By the 1300s the kingdom of Alwa was dissolved, and Old Dongola fell in 1323 to Kanz ed-Dawla.[13] Nubia remained independent until it was gradually reduced by Egyptian Mamluk rulers and Bedouin incursions from the fourteenth century to the sixteenth. By the end of the medieval period Nubia was in a very different state: the centralized government had dissolved, Christianity was no longer an organized religion, there was no foreign trade, and all artistic traditions had disappeared.[14] The heyday of empire was long gone.

Islamic Nubia

The Islamization of Sudan was gradual and culminated in the sixteenth century with the rise of the Funj Sultanate. During this time conflicts with the Ottoman Empire resulted in the loss of Nubian territory as far as the Third Cataract region when the Ottoman forces occupied Sai Island.[15] Simultaneously, Darfur saw the rise of Islam with the presence of both the Sunni and Sufi sects, the former focusing on orthodox traditions and the mosque, and the latter emphasizing the Muslim holy men.[16]

Muhammad Ali Pasha conquered Sudan in the name of the Ottoman Empire in 1821. Following years of fighting, Khartoum officially fell in 1885. Muhammad Ahmed became the Mahdi of Sudan, but he died only six months after the conquest of Khartoum. The Mahdist state was overthrown by the British in the 1890s in order to secure the area for the planned Aswan Dam. The campaign was led by Herbert Kitchener in a series of battles leading up to the Battle of Omdurman on 2 September 1898; he was subsequently appointed the first governor-general in 1899.[17]

The Egyptian revolution in July 1952 paved the way for Sudanese independence, which was granted on 1 January 1956. At this time the flags of Egypt and Britain were lowered, and the new flag of an independent Sudan was raised.[18] However, independence did not always guarantee peace and years of civil war raged between the north and south. In 2011 a referendum was held from 9 to 15 January to determine whether Sudan would remain a single country or divide into northern and southern states, and on 9 July the Republic of South Sudan was officially recognized.

Following years of economic sanctions by the United States, the elimination of bread and petroleum subsidies, and a rapid devaluation of currency due to oil revenue losses after the independence of South Sudan in 2011, the people of North Sudan began protesting in the streets of Khartoum in December 2018. The protests reached their height on 6 April 2019, the anniversary of the 1985 removal of Jaafar Nimeiri, the country's previous dictatorial president. Protesters began calling for the resignation of Omar al-Bashir following his thirty-year regime. He was arrested and removed from the presidential palace on 17 April 2019. Sadly this did not mark the beginning of a democratic society as a coup, led by General Abdel Fattah al-Burhan, overthrew the transitional government on 25 October 2021 and the civilian prime minister, Abdalla Hamdok, was placed under house arrest. The citizens resumed their protests in the hope of stability and peace for their beloved Sudan. On 21 November, under pressure from Saudi Arabia, the United Arab Emirates, the USA and the UK, the military agreed to a renewal of the transition to civilian rule, the release of political prisoners and the reinstatement of Abdalla Hamdok. On 2 January 2022, Hamdok resigned as prime minister and protests resumed once again.

Today we are experiencing a shift in society that is making us more aware of the histories and influences that African and African diaspora communities have had on the development of our collective consciousness. Given the current social climate and the increased focus on Black communities, connections with the strength and power of Africa are becoming even more important. My hope is that this book has provided another stepping stone on the path to bringing these peoples and cultures back into the foreground, and reminding us that Black lives have always mattered and have had a lasting impact on our world.

■‍‍‍‍ REFERENCES

1 THE 'LOST' LAND OF NUBIA

1 David O'Connor, 'The Locations of Yam and Kush and Their Historical Implications', *Journal of the American Research Center in Egypt*, XXIII (1986), pp. 27–50; Elmar Edel, 'Inscriften des Alten Reiches XI. Nachtrage zu den Reiseberichten des *ḥrw-ḫwif*', *Zeitschrift für ägyptische Sprache und Altertumskunde*, LXXXV (1960), pp. 18–23; Jean Yoyotte, 'Pour une localization du pays de Iam', *Bulletin de l'Institut Français d'Archéologie Orientale*, LII (1953), pp. 173–8; D. M. Dixon, 'The Land of Yam', *Journal of Egyptian Archaeology*, XLIV (1958), pp. 40–55; Julien Cooper, 'Reconsidering the Location of Yam', *Journal of the American Research Center in Egypt*, XLVIII (2012), p. 21.

2 Julien Cooper, 'Toponymic Strata in Ancient Nubia until the Common Era', *Dowato*, IV (2017), p. 200.

3 Ibid.

4 Dietrich D. Klemm, Rosemarie Klemm and Andreas Murr, 'Ancient Gold Mining in the Eastern Desert of Egypt and the Nubian Desert of Sudan', in *Egypt and Nubia: Gifts of the Desert*, ed. Renée Friedman (London, 2002), pp. 215–31.

5 William Y. Adams, 'Ecology and Economy in the Empire of Kush', *Zeitschrift für ägyptische Sprache und Altertumskunde*, CVIII (1981), pp. 1–11 (p. 8).

6 William Y. Adams, *Meroitic North and South: A Study in Cultural Contrasts* (Berlin, 1976), p. 149; Adams, 'Ecology and Economy', p. 5; Graham Connah, *African Civilizations* (Cambridge, 1987), p. 62; Derek A. Welsby, *The Kingdom of Kush: The Napatan and Meroitic Empires* (London, 1996), pp. 175–6; K. A. Ahmed, 'Economy and Environment in the Empire of Kush', *Meroitica*, XV (1999), pp. 302–4.

7 John Lewis Burckhardt, *Travels in Nubia*, 2nd edn (New York, 1978), p. 290.

8 Ibid., p. 307.

9 For the use of natron in temple rituals, see Rosalie A. David, *Religious Ritual at Abydos (c. 1300 BC)* (Warminster, 1973) and Katherine Eaton, *Ancient Egyptian Temple Ritual: Performance, Pattern, and Practice* (London, 2013).

10 Bogdon Żurawski, 'Dongola Reach: The Southern Dongola Reach Survey, 1998/1999', *Polish Archaeology in the Mediterranean*, XI (2000), p. 218. It is uncertain whether the salty deposits at Sonijat were substantial enough to be mined, or if they were simply the result of salinization of the ground. It is to be hoped that further excavation of the temple and its surrounding area will yield additional evidence in these deposits and on their use at Sonijat.

11 Horace Leonard, trans., *The Geography of Strabo* (Cambridge, MA, 1967), p. 145.

12 Burckhardt, *Travels*, p. 246.

13 Ibid.

14 W. Paul Van Pelt, 'Revising Egypto-Nubian Relations in New Kingdom Lower Nubia: From Egyptianization to Cultural Entanglement', *Cambridge Archaeological Journal*, XXIII/3 (2013), pp. 523–50; Michele Buzon, Stuart Tyson Smith and Antonio Simonetti, 'Entanglement and the Formation of the Ancient Nubian Napatan State', *American Anthropologist*, CXVIII/2 (2016), pp. 284–300.

15 Geoff Emberling, 'Ethnicity in Complex Societies: Archaeological Perspectives', *Journal of Archaeological Research*, V/4 (1997), pp. 295–344; Stuart Tyson Smith, *Wretched Kush: Ethnic Identities and Boundaries in Egypt's Nubian Empire* (New York, 2003).

16 Buzon, Smith and Simonetti, 'Entanglement', p. 296.

17 Angelika Lohwasser, *The Kushite Cemetery of Sanam: A Non-Royal Burial Ground of the Nubian Capital, c. 800-600 B.C.* (London, 2010); Michaela Binder, Neal Spencer and Marie Millet, 'Cemetery D at Amara West: The Ramesside Period and Its Aftermath', *Sudan and Nubia*, XIV (2010), pp. 25–44.

18 Van Pelt, 'Revising Egypto-Nubian Relations', p. 531.

2 FROM NOMADS TO LEADERS

1 William Y. Adams, *Nubia: Corridor to Africa* (Princeton, NJ, 1977), pp. 109–10; Elena A. A. Garcea, 'The Palaeolithic and Mesolithic', in *Sudan Ancient Treasures: Recent Discoveries from the Sudan National Museum*, ed. Derek A. Welsby and Julie R. Anderson, exh. cat., British Museum (London, 2004), p. 23.

2 Garcea, 'Palaeolithic and Mesolithic', p. 23; Isabella Caneva, 'The Saggai Region', in *Sudan Ancient Treasures*, pp. 29–30.

3 Caneva, 'The Saggai Region', p. 29.

4 Adams, *Nubia*, p. 113; Frederike Jesse, 'The Neolithic', in *Sudan Ancient Treasures*, p. 37.

5 Marjorie M. Fisher, 'The History of Nubia', in *Ancient Nubia: African Kingdoms on the Nile*, ed. Marjorie M. Fisher, Peter Lacovara, Salima Ikram and Sue D'Auria (New York and Cairo, 2012), p. 13; Jesse, 'Neolithic', p. 40.

6 Adams, *Nubia*, p. 110; for a discussion on the development of agriculture during the Neolithic period, see László Török, *Between Two Worlds:*

The Frontier Region between Ancient Nubia and Egypt, 3700 BC–500 AD (Leiden, 2009), pp. 25–6.

7 Jesse, 'Neolithic', p. 39.

8 Adams, *Nubia*, p. 113.

9 Jesse, 'Neolithic', pp. 37–8; Jacques Reinold, 'Kadruka', in *Sudan Ancient Treasures*, p. 46.

10 Fisher, 'History of Nubia', p. 13; Jesse, 'Neolithic', p. 38.

11 Giulia D'Ercole, 'Seventy Years of Pottery Studies in the Archaeology of Mesolithic and Neolithic Sudan', *African Archaeological Review*, XXXVIII (2021), pp. 345–72 (p. 348); Reinold, 'Kadruka', in *Sudan Ancient Treasures*, pp. 43–4; Lech Krzyżaniak, 'Kadero', in *Sudan Ancient Treasures*, p. 50.

12 Fisher, 'History of Nubia', p. 13; Jesse, 'Neolithic', p. 40. Stelae were discovered at Kadruka, sacrifices at el-Ghaba and el-Kadada, and bucrania at el-Ghaba, Kadruka and el-Kadada.

13 Török, *Between Two Worlds*, p. 41; Maria Carmela Gatto, 'The Nubian A-Group: A Reassessment', *Archéonil*, XVI (2006), pp. 67–8.

14 Gatto, 'The Nubian A-Group', p. 69.

15 Ibid., p. 70.

16 Bruce Beyer Williams, *Excavations between Abu Simbel and the Sudan Frontier*, vol. III: *The A-Group Royal Cemetery at Qustul: Cemetery L* (Chicago, IL, 1986).

17 Claire Somaglino and Pierre Tallet, 'Gebel Sheikh Suleiman: A First Dynasty Relief after All . . .', *Archéo-Nil*, XXV (2015), pp. 123–34.

18 Ibid., pp. 127–8.

19 George Reisner identified another culture between the A-Group and C-Group, which he classified as the 'B-Group'. All of his evidence was centred around the cemeteries as no settlement sites were identified and dated to this period. At this point there is little evidence that Reisner's 'B-Group' cemeteries should be considered those of a distinct cultural group. Instead, they are now considered to be lower-status members of the A-Group. For discussions about the 'B-Group', see H. S. Smith, 'The Nubian B-Group', *KUSH: Journal of the Sudan Antiquities Service*, XIV/1 (1966), pp. 69–124, and H. S. Smith, 'The Development of the "A-Group" Culture in Northern Lower Nubia', in *Egypt and Africa: Nubia from Prehistory to Islam*, ed. W. V. Davies (London, 1991), pp. 92–111.

20 James Henry Breasted, *Ancient Records of Egypt*, vol. I: *The First through the Seventeenth Dynasties* (Chicago, IL, 1906), p. 66.

21 Török, *Between Two Worlds*, p. 64.

22 Adams, *Nubia*, p. 147; Bruce G. Trigger, *History and Settlement in Lower Nubia* (New Haven, CT, 1965), pp. 97–8.

23 Adams, *Nubia*, p. 149.

24 Ibid., p. 144; Török, *Between Two Worlds*, p. 71.

25 Stuart Tyson Smith, 'Askut and the Role of the Second Cataract Forts', *Journal of the American Research Center in Egypt*, XXVIII (1991), pp. 107–32.

26 Matthieu Honegger, 'The Pre-Kerma Settlement: New Elements Throw Light on the Rise of the First Nubian Kingdom', in *Nubian*

Studies 1998: Proceedings of the Ninth Conference of the International Society of Nubian Studies, ed. Timothy Kendall (Boston, MA, 2004), p. 83; Matthieu Honegger, 'The Pre-Kerma Period', in *Sudan Ancient Treasures*, p. 66.

27 Honegger, 'Pre-Kerma Period', pp. 64–5; Honegger, 'Pre-Kerma Settlement', p. 89.

28 Honegger, 'Pre-Kerma Period', pp. 65 and 89; Matthieu Honegger, 'Kerma: L'agglomération pré-Kerma', *Genava*, XLV (1997), p. 115.

29 Honegger, 'Pre-Kerma Period', p. 65.

30 Honegger, 'Pre-Kerma Settlement', p. 89.

31 Honegger, 'Pre-Kerma Period', p. 64.

32 Ibid., cat. nos 51 and 54.

33 Honegger, 'Pre-Kerma Settlement', p. 88.

34 George Andrew Reisner, *Excavations at Kerma: Joint Egyptian Expedition of Harvard University and the Boston Museum of Fine Arts*, 2 vols (Cambridge, MA, 1923).

35 Charles Bonnet, 'The Kingdom of Kerma', in *Sudan: Ancient Kingdoms of the Nile*, ed. Dietrich Wildung (Paris and New York, 1997), p. 89.

36 Ibid., p. 94.

37 Bonnet, 'Kerma', in *Sudan Ancient Treasures*, p. 79.

38 Charles Bonnet, 'Excavations at the Nubian Royal Town of Kerma: 1975–91', *Antiquity*, LXVI (1992), pp. 611–25 (pp. 614–16).

39 Ibid., p. 616.

40 Charles Bonnet, Jacques Reinold, Brigitte Gratien, Bruno Marcolongo and Nicola Surian, 'Les fouilles archéologiques de Kerma (Soudan): Rapport préliminaire sur les campagnes de 1991–1992 et de 1992–1993', *Genava*, XLI (1993), p. 3.

41 Ibid., p. 4.

42 Ibid., p. 5.

43 Bonnet, 'Kingdom of Kerma', p. 90.

44 Bonnet, 'Kerma Culture', p. 75.

45 Francis Geus, 'Funerary Culture', in *Sudan Ancient Kingdoms*, p. 278.

46 Matthieu Honegger and Camille Fallet, 'Archers' tombs of Kerma Ancien', *Kerma: Documents de la mission archéologique suisse au Soudan*, VI (2015), pp. 16–30.

47 Subsidiary burials, which have been interpreted as human sacrifices, were also found in elite and royal tombs beginning in the Classic Kerma period. For an extensive study of the Classic Kerma burials, their contents, and the evidence for social stratification and human sacrifice, see Elizabeth Minor, 'The Use of Egyptian and Egyptianizing Material Culture in Nubian Burials of the Classic Kerma Period', PhD thesis, University of California, Berkeley, 2012.

48 Elizabeth Minor, 'One More for the Road: Beer, Sacrifice and Commemoration in Ancient Nubian Burials of the Classic Kerma Period', in *Current Research in Egyptology 2017: Proceedings of the Eighteenth Annual Symposium*, ed. Ilaria Incordino et al. (Oxford, 2018), p. 126.

49 Ibid., p. 127.
50 Bonnet, 'Kerma', in *Sudan Ancient Treasures*, p. 80.
51 Minor, 'One More for the Road', p. 127.
52 Bonnet, 'Kerma Culture', p. 75.
53 Bonnet, 'Kingdom of Kerma', p. 92.
54 Christian Knoblauch and Peter Lacovara, 'Nubian Ceramics', in *Ancient Nubia: African Kingdoms on the Nile*, ed. Fisher et al., p. 203.
55 Brigitte Gratien, 'L'Habitat 2 de Gism el-Arba: Rapport préliminaire sur un centre de stockage Kerma?', *Cahier de Recherches de l'Institut de Papyrologie et d'Egyptologie de Lille*, XXIII (2003), pp. 29–43; Brigitte Gratien, 'Some Rural Settlements at Gism el-Arba in the Northern Dongola Reach', *Sudan and Nubia*, III (1999), pp. 10–12.
56 Louis Chaix, 'New Data about Rural Economy in the Kerma Culture: The Site of Gism-el-Arba (Sudan)', *Studies in African Archaeology*, IX (2007), pp. 25–38.

3 Nubia and Egypt

1 Nigel C. Strudwick, *Texts from the Pyramid Age* (Atlanta, GA, 2005), pp. 352–7.
2 Ibid., p. 357.
3 Ibid., pp. 330–33.
4 Ibid., p. 333.
5 Ibid., pp. 336–8.
6 László Török, *Between Two Worlds: The Frontier Region between Ancient Nubia and Egypt, 3700 BC–500 AD* (Leiden, 2009), p. 84; Kate Liszka and Bryan Kraemer, 'Evidence for Administration of the Nubian Fortresses in the Late Middle Kingdom: P. Ramesseum 18', *Journal of Egyptian History*, IX/2 (2016), p. 188.
7 Denise M. Doxey, Rita E. Freed and Lawrence M. Berman, *Arts of Ancient Nubia* (Boston, MA, 2018), pp. 134–5.
8 Ibid., p. 136.
9 William Kelly Simpson, ed., *The Literature of Ancient Egypt: An Anthology of Stories, Instructions, Stelae, Autobiographies, and Poetry*, 3rd edn (New Haven, CT, and London, 2003), p. 338.
10 Bryan Kraemer and Kate Liszka, 'Evidence for Administration of the Nubian Fortresses in the Late Middle Kingdom: The Semna Dispatches', *Journal of Egyptian History*, IX/1 (2016), 1–65 (pp. 14–15, 45).
11 Ibid., p. 30.
12 Liszka and Kraemer, 'P. Ramesseum 18', pp. 161–6, 190–91.
13 Marjorie M. Fisher, 'The History of Nubia', in *Ancient Nubia: African Kingdoms on the Nile*, ed. Marjorie M. Fisher, Peter Lacovara, Salima Ikram and Sue D'Auria (New York and Cairo, 2012), p. 22; Liszka and Kraemer, 'P. Ramesseum 18', pp. 194–5.
14 Török, *Between Two Worlds*, p. 59.
15 Doxey, Freed and Berman, *Arts of Ancient Nubia*, p. 140.

16 Vivian Davies, 'Kush in Egypt: A New Historical Inscription', *Sudan and Nubia*, VII (2003), pp. 52–4 (p. 52).

17 Ibid., p. 53.

18 Elizabeth Minor, 'The Use of Egyptian and Egyptianizing Material Culture in Classic Kerma Burials: Winged Sun Discs', in *Les Produits de luxe au Proche-Orient ancien, aux âges du Bronze et du Fer*, ed. Michèle Casanova and Martin Feldman (Paris, 2014), p. 227.

19 Ibid., pp. 231–2; Elizabeth Minor, 'Decolonizing Reisner: A Case Study of a Classic Kerma Female Burial for Reinterpreting Early Nubian Archaeological Collections through Digital Archival Resources', in *Nubian Archaeology in the XXIst Century: Proceedings of the Thirteenth International Conference for Nubian Studies* (Leuven, 2018), p. 259, fig. 8.

20 Doxey, Freed and Berman, *Arts of Ancient Nubia*, p. 29.

21 Labib Habachi, *The Second Stela of Kamose and His Struggle against the Hyksos Ruler and His Capital* (Glückstadt, 1972).

22 Simpson, *The Literature of Ancient Egypt*, p. 346.

23 David O'Connor, 'New Kingdom and Third Intermediate Period, 1552–664 BC', in *Ancient Egypt: A Social History*, ed. Bruce G. Trigger et al. (Cambridge, 1983), p. 262.

24 Nina de Garis Davies and Alan H. Gardiner, *The Tomb of Huy: Viceroy of Nubia in the Reign of Tut'ankhamūn (No. 40)* (London, 1926).

25 Robert Morkot, 'From Conquered to Conquerer: The Organization of Nubia in the New Kingdom and the Kushite Administration of Egypt', in *Ancient Egyptian Administration*, ed. Juan Carlos Moreno García (Leiden, 2013), p. 916.

26 Florence Doyen, 'The New Kingdom Town on Sai Island (Northern Sudan)', *Sudan and Nubia*, XIII (2009), pp. 17–20 (p. 17); Julia Budka, 'The Early New Kingdom at Sai Island: Preliminary Results Based on the Pottery Analysis (4th Season 2010)', *Sudan and Nubia*, XV (2011), pp. 23–33 (pp. 24, 29).

27 Doyen, 'New Kingdom Town on Sai Island', p. 18; Budka, 'Sai Island, Pottery Analysis', p. 23; Florence Doyen, 'Sai Island New Kingdom Town (Northern Sudan): 3rd and 4th Seasons (2009–2010)', in *The Fourth Cataract and Beyond: Proceedings of the Twelfth International Conference for Nubian Studies*, ed. Julie R. Anderson and Derek A. Welsby (Leuven, 2014), p. 369.

28 Budka, 'Sai Island, Pottery Analysis', p. 23.

29 Julia Budka and Florence Doyen, 'Life in New Kingdom Towns in Upper Nubia: New Evidence from Recent Excavations on Sai Island', *Ägypten und Levante/Egypt and the Levant*, XXII/XXIII (2012/13), pp. 167–208 (p. 182).

30 Doyen, 'New Kingdom Town on Sai Island', p. 18; Budka and Doyen, 'Life in New Kingdom Towns', p. 171.

31 Doyen, 'New Kingdom Town on Sai Island', pp. 18–19; Budka, 'Sai Island, Pottery Analysis', p. 24; Budka and Doyen, 'Life in New Kingdom Towns', pp. 171–2.

32 Kate Spence et al., 'Sesebi 2011', *Sudan and Nubia*, XV (2011), pp. 34–9 (p. 38); Derek Welsby, 'Excavations at Kawa, 2009–10', *Sudan and Nubia*, XIV (2010), pp. 48–55 (p. 52). Spence et al., 'Sesebi 2011', p. 34.

33 Dietrich D. Klemm, Rosemarie Klemm and Andreas Murr, 'Ancient Gold Mining in the Eastern Desert of Egypt and the Nubian Desert of Sudan', in *Egypt and Nubia: Gifts of the Desert*, ed. Renée Friedman (London, 2002), p. 216.

34 Kate Spence and Pamela Rose, 'Fieldwork at Sesebi 2010', in *The Fourth Cataract and Beyond*, ed. Anderson and Welsby, p. 414.

35 Kate Spence et al., 'Fieldwork at Sesebi, 2009', *Sudan and Nubia*, XIII (2009), pp. 38–46 (p. 42); Spence and Rose, 'Sesebi 2010', p. 412.

36 Spence et al., 'Sesebi 2009', p. 42; Spence et al., 'Sesebi 2011', p. 37.

37 Neal Spencer, Anna Stevens and Michaela Binder, *Amara West: Living in Egyptian Nubia* (London, 2014), p. 10.

38 Ibid., p. 10; Neal Spencer, 'Amara West: Considerations on Urban Life in Colonial Kush', in *The Fourth Cataract and Beyond*, ed. Anderson and Welsby, p. 459.

39 Spencer, Stevens and Binder, *Amara West*, p. 14.

40 Neal Spencer, 'Cemeteries and a Late Ramesside Suburb at Amara West', *Sudan and Nubia*, XIII (2009), pp. 47–61 (p. 47); Spencer, Stevens and Binder, *Amara West*, p. 15.

41 Spencer, 'Cemeteries and a Late Ramesside Suburb', p. 47; Spencer, Stevens and Binder, *Amara West*, p. 17; Spencer, 'Amara West: Considerations', p. 459.

42 Spencer, 'Cemeteries and a Late Ramesside Suburb', p. 56; Spencer, 'Amara West: Considerations', p. 468.

43 Spencer, 'Cemeteries and a Late Ramesside Suburb', p. 55.

44 Ibid.; Richard B. Parkinson and Neal Spencer, 'The *Teaching of Amenemhat* at Amara West', *Egyptian Archaeology*, XXXV (2009), pp. 25–7 (p. 27); Spencer, 'Amara West: Considerations', p. 481.

45 Richard B. Parkinson and Neal Spencer, 'Reading Amenemhat in Upper Nubia', in Spencer, Stevens and Binder, *Amara West*, p. 18.

46 Charles Bonnet and Dominique Valbelle, 'Kerma, Dokki Gel', in *Sudan Ancient Treasures: Recent Discoveries from the Sudan National Museum*, ed. Derek A. Welsby and Julie R. Anderson, exh. cat., British Museum (London, 2004), p. 109.

47 Charles Bonnet, *The Black Kingdom of the Nile* (Cambridge, MA, and London, 2019), p. 72.

48 Bonnet and Valbelle, 'Kerma, Dokki Gel', p. 109.

49 David N. Edwards, *The Nubian Past: An Archaeology of the Sudan* (Abingdon and New York, 2004), p. 108.

50 Renée Friedman, Margaret Judd and Joel D. Irish, 'The Nubian Cemetery at Hierakonpolis, Egypt: Results of the 2007 Season', *Sudan and Nubia*, XI (2007), pp. 57–71.

51 Ibid., pp. 60–61.

52 Eric Doret, 'Ankhtifi and the Description of his Tomb at Mo'alla', in *For*

His Ka: Essays Offered in Memory of Klaus Baer, ed. David P. Silverman (Chicago, IL, 1994), pp. 79–86.

4 WHEN NUBIA RULED THE (ANCIENT) WORLD

1 Irene Liverani, 'Hillat el-Arab', in *Sudan Ancient Treasures: Recent Discoveries from the Sudan National Museum*, ed. Derek A. Welsby and Julie R. Anderson, exh. cat., British Museum (London, 2004), pp. 138–47; Irene Vincentelli, *Hillat el-Arab: The Joint Sudanese–Italian Expedition in the Napatan Region, Sudan* (Oxford, 2006).

2 Robert Morkot, *The Black Pharaohs: Egypt's Nubian Rulers* (London, 2000), p. 158.

3 Sarah M. Schellinger, 'Victory Stela of Pianki', in *Milestone Documents*, ed. Brian Bonhomme (Dallas, TX, 2014), pp. 91–107.

4 Derek Welsby, *Kingdom of Kush: The Napatan and Meroitic Empires* (London, 1996), p. 26; Jean Revez, 'The Metaphorical Use of the Kinship Term *sn* "Brother"', *Journal of the American Research Center in Egypt*, XL (2003), pp. 123–31; Samia Dafa'alla, 'Succession in the Kingdom of Napata, 900–300 BC', *International Journal of African Historical Studies*, XXVI (1993), pp. 167–74 (p. 170).

5 Kenneth A. Kitchen, *The Third Intermediate Period in Egypt (1100–650 BC)* (Oxford, 2004), p. 385.

6 Tormod Eide, Tomas Hägg, Richard Holton Pierce and László Török, eds, *Fontes Historiae Nubiorum: Textual Sources for the History of the Middle Nile Region between the Eighth Century BC and the Sixth Century AD*, vol. I: *From the Eighth to the Mid-Fifth Century BC* (Bergen, 1994), pp. 139 and 153; subsequently FHN I. For an extensive study of Taharqo's reign, see Jeremy Pope, *The Double Kingdom under Taharqo: Studies in the History of Kush and Egypt, c. 690–664 BC* (Leiden, 2014).

7 FHN I, pp. 150–51. Parentheses interjecting into quotes are direct from the sources whereas square brackets indicate the author's own insertions.

8 Ibid., p. 152.

9 László Török, *The Kingdom of Kush: Handbook of the Napatan-Meroitic Civilization* (Leiden, 1997), p. 172.

10 Ibid., pp. 180–81; David N. Edwards, *The Nubian Past: An Archaeology of the Sudan* (New York and Abingdon, 2004), p. 121.

11 Török, *Kingdom of Kush*, p. 172.

12 Ibid., p. 186.

13 FHN I, pp. 221–2.

14 The 'B' designation is for Barkal as Jebel Barkal is the modern name of the site.

15 Török, *Kingdom of Kush*, p. 366.

16 Bogdan Żurawski, 'Pliny's "Tergedum" Discovered', *Sudan and Nubia*, II (1998), p. 80.

17 Török, *Kingdom of Kush*, p. 373.

18 Ibid.

19 Thomas O. Reimer, 'The Presentation of Gold in the Reliefs of the Eastern Staircase of the Apadana in Persepolis', *Iranian Journal of Archaeological Studies*, III/1 (2013), pp. 57–63 (pp. 60–62).

20 John Garstang and A. H. Sayce, 'Second Interim Report on the Excavations at Meroe in Ethiopia', *Liverpool Annals of Archaeology and Anthropology*, IV (1912), p. 49; László Török, with I. Hofmann and I. Nagy, *Meroe City: An Ancient African Capital; John Garstang's Excavations in Sudan, Part One: Text* (London, 1997), p. 154.

21 Richard Lobban, 'Greeks, Nubians and Mapping the Ancient Nile', in *Nubian Studies 1998: Proceedings of the Ninth Conference of the International Society of Nubian Studies*, ed. Timothy Kendall (Boston, MA, 2004), p. 341.

22 Ibid., p. 342.

23 Tormod Eide, Tomas Hägg, Richard Holton Pierce and László Török, eds, *Fontes Historiae Nubiorum: Textual Sources for the History of the Middle Nile Region between the Eighth Century BC and the Sixth Century AD*, vol. II: *From the Mid-Fifth Century to the First Century BC* (Bergen, 1996), pp. 691, 695–9; subsequently *FHN* II; Stanley Burstein, 'Rome and Kush: A New Interpretation', in *Nubian Studies 1998: Proceedings of the Ninth Conference of the International Society of Nubian Studies*, ed. Timothy Kendall (Boston, MA, 2004), p. 16.

24 *FHN* II, pp. 689ff.

25 Aminata Sackho-Autissier, 'La Guerre entre Méroé et Rome, 25–21 av. J.-C.', in *Méroé: Un Empire sur le Nil*, ed. Michel Baud (Paris, 2010), p. 73.

26 Ibid.

27 Burstein, 'Rome and Kush', p. 17.

28 László Török, *Hellenizing Art in Ancient Nubia, 300 BC–AD 250, and Its Egyptian Models: A Study in 'Acculturation'* (Leiden, 2011), p. 304.

29 Ibid., p. 306.

30 Loredana Sist, 'Motivi ellenistici nell'architettura meroitica: nuove scoperte a Napata', in *Acta Nubica: Proceedings of the X International Conference of Nubian Studies*, ed. Isabella Caneva and Alessandro Roccati (Rome, 2006), p. 475; Alessando Roccati, 'L'Hellénisme dans l'architecture et la décoration des palais de Napata', in *Méroé*, ed. Baud (Paris, 2010), p. 96.

31 Sist, 'Motivi ellenistici', p. 476.

32 Kathryn A. Bard, Rodolfo Fattovich, Andrea Manzo and Cinzia Perlingieri, 'Aksum Origins, Kassala and Upper Nubia: New Evidence from Bieta Giyorgis, Aksum', *Archéologie du Nil Moyen*, IX (2002), p. 34; Rodolfo Fattovich, 'The Development of Ancient States in the Northern Horn of Africa, c. 3000 BC–AD 1000: An Archaeological Outline', *Journal of World Prehistory*, XXIII (2010), pp. 145–75 (p. 158).

33 Rodolfo Fattovich, 'At the Periphery of the Empire: The Gash Delta (Eastern Sudan)', in *Egypt and Africa: Nubia from Prehistory to Islam*, ed. W. V. Davies (London, 1991), p. 45; Bard et al., 'Aksum Origins', p. 35; Fattovich, 'Development of Ancient States', p. 155.

34 Fattovich, 'At the Periphery of the Empire', p. 41.

35 Bard et al., 'Aksum Origins', p. 37.

36 Fattovich, 'Development of Ancient States', p. 157.

37 Rodolfo Fattovich, 'The Problem of Sudanese–Ethiopian Contacts in Antiquity: Status Quaestionis and Current Trends of Research', in *Nubian Studies: Proceedings of the Symposium for Nubian Studies*, ed. J. Martin Plumley (Warminster, 1982), p. 76.

38 Pawel Wolf, 'Essay über den meroitischen Eklektizismus in Musawwarat es Sufra, oder: Woher stammt der meroitische Einraumtempel?', in *Ein Forscherleben zwischen den Welten: zum 80. Geburtstag von Steffen Wenig*, ed. Angelika Lohwasser and Pawel Wolf (Berlin, 2014), p. 358.

39 Welsby, *Kingdom of Kush*, p. 190.

40 Claude Rilly and Alex de Voogt, *The Meroitic Language and Writing System* (Cambridge, 2012).

41 Tormod Eide, Tomas Hägg, Richard Holton Pierce and László Török, eds, *Fontes Historiae Nubiorum: Textual Sources for the History of the Middle Nile Region Between the Eighth Century BC and the Sixth Century AD*, vol. III: *From the First to the Sixth Century AD* (Bergen, 1998), pp. 1066ff; subsequently *FHN III*.

42 Ibid., pp. 1094ff.

5 THE NUBIAN PANTHEON

1 Caroline M. Rocheleau, *Amun Temples in Nubia: A Typological Study of New Kingdom, Napatan and Meroitic Temples* (Oxford, 2008).

2 The species of ram associated with the god Khnum was *Ovis longipes palaeoaegyptiacus* and was attested in Egypt as early as the Predynastic period. The ram species associated with the god Amun was *Ovis platyra aegyptiaca*, which was known from the Middle Kingdom, approximately Dynasty 12, onwards. These species are differentiated by the type of horns, the former having horns that are wavy and stretch horizontally above the head, and the latter having horns that curve down and around the ears towards the mouth. Khnum was also closely associated with water, particularly the source of the Nile, as that was under his domain. Rams of the *Ovis platyra aegyptiaca* were used to find sources of water in the desert: Katja Goebs, '"Receive the Henu – that You May Shine Forth in it like Akhty": Feathers, Horns and the Composite Symbolism of Egyptian Composite Crowns', in *Königtum, Staat und Gesellschaft Früher Hochkulturen 4.4: 7th Symposium on Egyptian Royal Ideology; Royal versus Divine Authority*, ed. Filip Coppens, Jiří Janák and Hana Vymazalová (Wiesbaden, 2015), p. 171.

3 Eleonora Y. Kormysheva, 'On the Origin and Evolution of the Amun Cult in Nubia', in *Nubian Studies 1998: Proceedings of the Ninth Conference of the International Society of Nubian Studies*, ed. Timothy Kendall (Boston, MA, 2004), p. 113.

4 *FHN I*, p. 77.

5 Ibid., pp. 198–200.

6 *FHN* II, pp. 442–3.

7 Ibid., p. 499; Emanuele M. Ciampini and Grażyna Bąkowska-Czerner, 'Meroitic Kingship and Water: The Case of Napata (B2200)', in *The Fourth Cataract and Beyond: Proceedings of the Twefth International Conference for Nubian Studies*, ed. Julie R. Anderson and Derek A. Welsby (Leuven, 2014), p. 696.

8 Ibid., p. 698.

9 John Garstang, W. J. Phythian-Adams and A. H. Sayce, 'Fifth Interim Report on the Excavations at Meroë in Ethiopia', *Liverpool Annals of Archaeology and Anthropology*, VII (1914–16), p. 12.

10 László Török, *Hellenizing Art in Ancient Nubia 300 BC–AD 250 and Its Egyptian Models: A Study in 'Acculturation'* (Leiden, 2011), p. 131.

11 *FHN* I, p. 36.

12 Ibid., p. 237.

13 László Török, 'Space, Temple, and Society: On the Built Worldview of the Twenty-Fifth Dynasty in Nubia', in *Acta Nubica: Proceedings of the X International Conference of Nubian Studies*, ed. Isabella Caneva and Alessandro Roccati (Rome, 2006), p. 233.

14 László Török, *The Image of the Ordered World in Ancient Nubian Art: The Construction of the Kushite Mind (800 BC–300 AD)* (Leiden, 2002), pp. 72–3.

15 Charles Bonnet and Dominique Valbelle, *The Nubian Pharaohs: Black Kings on the Nile* (Cairo, 2006), p. 38.

16 Angelika Lohwasser, 'Neujahr in Nubien', in *Ein Forscherleben zwischen den Welten: zum 80. Geburtstag von Steffen Wenig*, ed. Angelika Lohwasser and Pawel Wolf (Berlin, 2014), p. 230.

17 Alan Gardiner, 'The Coronation of King Haremhab', *Journal of Egyptian Archaeology*, XXXIX (1953), pp. 13–31.

18 David O'Connor, 'Beloved of Maat, the Horizon of Re: The Royal Palace in New Kingdom Egypt', in *Ancient Egyptian Kingship*, ed. David O'Connor and David P. Silverman (Leiden, 1995), p. 278; Giulia Pagliari, 'Function and Significance of Ancient Egyptian Royal Palaces from the Middle Kingdom to the Saite Period', PhD thesis, University of Birmingham and La 'Sapienza', University of Rome, 2012, pp. 232–75.

19 Timothy Kendall, 'Why Did Taharqa Build His Tomb at Nuri?', in *Between the Cataracts: Proceedings of the 11th Conference for Nubian Studies, Part One: Main Papers*, ed. Włodzimierz Godlewski and Adam Łajtar, Polish Archaeology in the Mediterranean, Supplement Series 2:1 (Warsaw, 2008), p. 125.

20 *FHN* I, pp. 196–7.

21 *FHN* II, p. 443.

22 Ibid., pp. 234–5.

23 Ibid., p. 401.

24   *FHN* I, p. 238.

25   Ibid., p. 401.

26   László Török, 'Ambulatory Kingship and Settlement History: A Study on the Contribution of Archaeology to Meroitic History', in *Études nubiennes: Conférence de Genève; Actes du VIIe Congrès international d'études nubiennes*, ed. Charles Bonnet (Geneva, 1992), p. 115; Jeremy Pope, *The Double Kingdom under Taharqo: Studies in the History of Kush and Egypt, c. 690–664 BC* (Leiden, 2014), pp. 38–40.

27   David O'Connor, 'City and Palace in New Kingdom Egypt', *Cahiers de Recherches de l'Institut de Papyrologie et d'Egyptologie de Lille*, XI (1989), pp. 73–87.

28   Ibid., p. 77.

29   Ibid., p. 483.

30   Janice W. Yellin, 'Egyptian Religion and Its Ongoing Impact on the Formation of the Napatan State. A Contribution to László Török's Main Paper: The Emergence of the Kingdom of Kush and her Myth of the State in the First Millennium BC', *Cahiers de Recherches de l'Institut de Papyrologie et d'Egyptologie de Lille*, XVII/1 (1995), p. 256.

31   Tomb number 52 at el-Kurru. MFA 24.928.

32   Janice Yellin, 'Nubian Religion', in *Ancient Nubia: African Kingdoms on the Nile*, ed. Marjorie M. Fisher, Peter Lacovara, Salima Ikram and Sue D'Auria (New York and Cairo, 2012), p. 134.

33   Ibid.

34   László Török, *The Kingdom of Kush: Handbook of the Napatan-Meroitic Civilization* (Leiden, 1997), p. 439; Török, *Image of the Ordered World*, p. 181.

35   Török, *Kingdom of Kush*, p. 439; Török, *Image of the Ordered World*, p. 182.

36   Török, *Kingdom of Kush*, pp. 440–41; Török, *Image of the Ordered World*, pp. 182, 186.

37   Yellin, 'Nubian Religion', p. 132.

38   Susan Kay Doll, 'Texts and Decoration on the Napatan Sarcophagi of Anlamani and Aspelta', PhD thesis, Brandeis University, 1978, p. 367.

39   F. J. Albers, 'The Pyramid Tombs of Tanutamen, Last Nubian Pharaoh and His Mother, Queen Qalhata', *KMT: A Modern Journal of Ancient Egypt*, XIV/2 (2003), pp. 52–63.

40   Eric A. Powell, 'Miniature Pyramids of Sudan', *Archaeology*, LXVI/4 (2013), p. 34.

41   David N. Edwards, *The Nubian Past: An Archaeology of the Sudan* (New York and Abingdon, 2004), p. 174.

42   Janice Yellin, 'The Role of Anubis in Meroitic Religion', in *Nubian Studies: Proceedings of the Symposium for Nubian Studies 1978*, ed. J. M. Plumley (Warminster, 1982), p. 229.

43   Janice Yellin, 'The Kushite Nature of Early Meroitic Mortuary Religion: A Pragmatic Approach to Osirian Beliefs', in *Ein Forscherleben zwischen*

den Welten: zum 80. Geburtstag von Steffen Wenig, ed. Angelika Lohwasser and Pawel Wolf (Berlin, 2014), pp. 395–404.

44 Ciampini and Bąkowska-Czerner, 'Meroitic Kingship', p. 699.

45 Ibid., p. 698.

46 Andrea Manzo, 'Apedemak and Dionysos: Further Remarks on the "Cult of the Grape" in Kush', *Sudan and Nubia*, x (2006), pp. 82–94 (p. 82).

6 MEROE AND THE *KANDAKES*

1 Solange Ashby, 'Dancing for Hathor: Nubian Women in Egyptian Cultic Life', *Dowato*, v (2018), pp. 63–90 (p. 67).

2 Mariam F. Ayad, 'The God's Wife of Amun: Origins and Rise to Power', in *The Routledge Companion to Women and Monarchy in the Ancient Mediterranean World*, ed. Elizabeth D. Carney and Sabine Müller (London, 2020), pp. 49–50.

3 Ibid., p. 49.

4 Ibid.

5 Ibid., p. 54.

6 Mariam F. Ayad, 'Some Thoughts on the Disappearance of the Office of the God's Wives of Amun', *Journal of the Society for the Study of Egyptian Antiquities*, XXVIII (2001), p. 9.

7 Elizabeth Minor, 'Decolonizing Reisner: A Case Study of a Classic Kerma Female Burial for Reinterpreting Early Nubian Archaeological Collections through Digital Archival Resources', in *Nubian Archaeology in the XXIst Century: Proceedings of the Thirteenth International Conference for Nubian Studies* (Leuven, 2018), pp. 251–62.

8 Ibid., p. 256.

9 László Török, *Birth of an Ancient African Kingdom: Kush and Her Myth of the State in the First Millennium BC* (Lille, 1995), pp. 48 and 99.

10 FHN I, pp. 36–7.

11 John Coleman Darnell, *The Inscription of Queen Katimala at Semna: Textual Evidence for the Origins of the Napatan State* (New Haven, CT, and London, 2006), p. ix.

12 Chris Bennett, 'Queen Karimala, Daughter of Osochor?', *Göttinger Miszellen*, CLXXIII (1999), pp. 7–8.

13 FHN I, p. 41.

14 Ibid.

15 Ibid., pp. 272–3.

16 László Török, *The Kingdom of Kush: Handbook of the Napatan-Meroitic Civilization* (Leiden, 1997), p. 369.

17 FHN I, p. 154.

18 Ibid., 223.

19 Dan'el Kahn, 'The Queen Mother in the Kingdom of Kush: Status, Power and Cultic Role', in *Teshura Le-Zafrira: Studies in the Bible, the History of Israel and the Ancient Near East Presented to Zafrira Ben-Barak*, ed. Mayer I. Gruber et al. (Beer Sheva, 2012), p. 61.

20 *FHN* II, pp. 507–8.

21 Ibid., p. 549.

22 Janice Yellin, 'The Chronology and Attribution of Royal Pyramids at Meroe and Gebel Barkal: Beg N 8, Beg N 12, Bar 5 and Bar 2', *Journal of Ancient Egyptian Interconnections*, VI/1 (2014), pp. 76–88; for the redating of Shanadakheto, see p. 80.

23 Joyce Haynes and Mimi Santini-Ritt, 'Women in Ancient Nubia', in *Ancient Nubia: African Kingdoms on the Nile*, ed. Marjorie M. Fisher, Peter Lacovara, Salima Ikram and Sue D'Auria (New York and Cairo, 2012), p. 182.

24 Aminata Sackho-Autissier, 'La Guerre entre Méroé et Rome, 25–21 av. J.-C.', in *Méroé: Un Empire sur le Nil*, ed. Michel Baud (Paris, 2010), p. 73; Pawel Wolf and Claude Rilly, 'Les Stèles de Hamadab', in *Méroé*, ed. Baud, p. 160; *FHN* II, pp. 719–23.

25 Ibid., p. 726.

26 Vlastimil Vrtal, 'The Palace of Queen Amanishakheto (WBN 100)', in *Wad Ben Naga: 1821–2013*, ed. Pavel Onderka et al. (Prague, 2013), p. 60.

27 Jean Vercoutter, 'Un Palais des "Candaces", contemporain d'Auguste (Fouilles à Wad-ban-Naga 1958–1960)', *Syria*, XXXIX (1962), pp. 278–9.

28 Yvonne M. Markowitz and Peter Lacovara, 'The Ferlini Treasure in Archaeological Perspective', *Journal of the American Research Center in Egypt*, XXXIII (1996), pp. 1–9.

29 Claude Rilly, 'Meroitische Texte aus Naga/ Meroitic Texts from Naga', in *Königsstadt Naga: Grabungen in der Wüste des Sudan/ Naga-Royal City: Excavations in the Desert of the Sudan*, ed. Karla Kröper, Sylvia Schoske and Dietrich Wildung (Munich and Berlin, 2011), p. 190.

30 Angelika Lohwasser, 'Queenship in Kush: Statue, Role and Ideology of Royal Women', *Journal of the American Research Center in Egypt*, XXXVIII (2001), pp. 61–76 (p. 63).

31 Shirin Jaafari, 'Here's the Story behind the Iconic Sudanese Woman in White', *The World*, 10 April 2019, https://theworld.org, accessed 1 September 2021.

7 Moving into the Iron Age

1 Nettie K. Adams, 'Influences from Abroad: The Evidence from the Textiles', in *Qasr Ibrim, Between Egypt and Africa: Studies in Cultural Exchange*, ed. J. van der Vliet and J. L. Hagen (Leuven, 2013), p. 67.

2 Michael Gervers, 'Cotton and Cotton Weaving in Meroitic Nubia and Medieval Ethiopia', *Textile History*, XXI/1 (1990), pp. 13–30 (p. 14).

3 Laurence P. Kirwan, 'A Survey of Nubian Origins', *Sudan Notes and Records*, xx/1 (1937), p. 51.

4 Gervers, 'Cotton and Cotton Weaving', p. 15.

5 László Török, *Between Two Worlds: The Frontier Region between Ancient Nubia and Egypt, 3700 BC–AD 500* (Leiden, 2009), pp. 411–26.

6 Ibid., pp. 391–411.

7 John Garstang and A. H. Sayce, 'Second Interim Report on the Excavations at Meroe in Ethiopia', *Liverpool Annals of Archaeology and Anthropology*, IV (1912), p. 55.

8 Jane Humphris, Michael F. Charlton, Jake Keen, Lee Sauder and Fareed Alshishani, 'Iron Smelting in Sudan: Experimental Archaeology at the Royal City of Meroe', *Journal of Field Archaeology*, XLIII/5 (2018), pp. 399–416 (p. 399).

9 Ibid., pp. 399–416.

10 Randi Haaland, 'Iron Working in an Indian Ocean Context', in *World of Iron*, ed. Jane Humphris and Thilo Rehren (London, 2013), p. 149.

11 Humphris et al., 'Iron Smelting', p. 400.

12 Haaland, 'Iron Working', p. 148.

13 Derek Welsby, *Kingdom of Kush: The Napatan and Meroitic Empires* (London, 1996), p. 170.

14 Gunnar Haaland and Randi Haaland, 'God of War, Worldly Ruler, and Craft Specialists in the Meroitic Kingdom of Sudan: Inferring Social Identity from Material Remains', *Journal of Social Archaeology*, VII/3 (2007), pp. 372–92 (p. 381).

15 Haaland, 'Iron Working', p. 151.

16 David W. Phillipson, *African Archaeology*, 3rd edn (Cambridge, 2005), p. 234.

17 Edwin E. Okafor, 'New Evidence on Early Iron-Smelting from Southwestern Nigeria', in *The Archaeology of Africa: Food, Metals and Towns*, ed. Thurstan Shaw, Paul Sinclair, Bassey Andah and Alex Okpoko (London and New York, 1993), p. 432.

18 Scopas Poggo, 'The Origins and Culture of Blacksmiths in Kuku Society of the Sudan, 1797–1955', *Journal of African Cultural Studies*, XVIII/2 (2006), pp. 169–86 (p. 172).

19 Ibid., p. 173.

20 Dr Scopas Poggo, Associate Professor of African American and African Studies at the Ohio State University and a proud member of the Kuku ethnic group, personal communication.

8 FROM NUBIA TO SUDAN

1 Francis Geus, 'Funerary Culture', in *Sudan Ancient Treasures: Recent Discoveries from the Sudan National Museum*, ed. Derek A. Welsby and Julie R. Anderson, exh. cat., British Museum (London, 2004), p. 282.

2 *FHN* III, pp. 1150–51.

3 Derek Welsby, *The Kingdom of Kush: The Napatan and Meroitic Empires* (London, 1996), p. 59.

4 Brenda J. Baker and Sarah M. Schellinger, 'The Qatar-Sudan Archaeological Project – Fourth Cataract: Preliminary Investigation of a Recently Discovered Fort in the ASU BONE Concession near el-Qinifab, Sudan', *Sudan and Nubia*, XXI (2017), pp. 169–76.

5 Julie R. Anderson, 'The Medieval Kingdoms of Nubia', in *Sudan Ancient Treasures*, ed. Welsby and Anderson, p. 202.

6 Ibid.

7 Ibid., p. 204.

8 William Y. Adams, 'Medieval Nubia: Another Golden Age', *Expedition*, XXXV/2 (1993), p. 32.

9 Geus, 'Funerary Culture', p. 282.

10 Adams, 'Medieval Nubia', p. 32.

11 Ibid., p. 35.

12 Ibid., p. 36.

13 Marjorie M. Fisher, 'The History of Nubia', in *Ancient Nubia: African Kingdoms on the Nile*, ed. Marjorie M. Fisher, Peter Lacovara, Salima Ikram and Sue D'Auria (New York and Cairo, 2012), p. 42.

14 Adams, 'Medieval Nubia', p. 39.

15 Intisar Soghayroun el-Zein, 'Islamic Archaeology in Sudan', in *Sudan Ancient Treasures*, ed. Welsby and Anderson, p. 240.

16 Ibid., p. 241.

17 P. M. Holt and M. W. Daly, *A History of the Sudan: From the Coming of Islam to the Present Day*, 5th edn (London, 2000), p. 102.

18 Ibid., p. 141.

BIBLIOGRAPHY

Adams, Nettie K., 'Influences from Abroad: The Evidence from the Textiles', in *Qasr Ibrim, Between Egypt and Africa: Studies in Cultural Exchange*, ed. J. van der Vliet and J. L. Hagen (Leuven, 2013), pp. 65–81

Adams, William Y., *Meroitic North and South: A Study in Cultural Contrasts* (Berlin, 1976)

——, *Nubia: Corridor to Africa* (Princeton, NJ, 1977)

——, 'Ecology and Economy in the Empire of Kush', *Zeitschrift für ägyptische Sprache und Altertumskunde*, CVIII (1981), pp. 1–11

——, 'Medieval Nubia: Another Golden Age', *Expedition*, XXXV/2 (1993), pp. 28–39

Ahmed, K. A., 'Economy and Environment in the Empire of Kush', *Meroitica*, XV (1999), pp. 291–311

Albers, F. J., 'The Pyramid Tombs of Tanutamen, Last Nubian Pharaoh and His Mother, Queen Qalhata', *KMT: A Modern Journal of Ancient Egypt*, XIV/2 (2003), pp. 52–63

Ashby, Solange, 'Dancing for Hathor: Nubian Women in Egyptian Cultic Life', *Dowato*, V (2018), pp. 63–90

Ayad, Mariam F., 'Some Thoughts on the Disappearance of the Office of the God's Wives of Amun', *Journal of the Society for the Study of Egyptian Antiquities*, XXVIII (2001), pp. 1–14

——, 'The God's Wife of Amun: Origins and Rise to Power', in *The Routledge Companion to Women and Monarchy in the Ancient Mediterranean World*, ed. Elizabeth D. Carney and Sabine Müller (London, 2020), pp. 47–60

Baker, Brenda J., and Sarah M. Schellinger, 'The Qatar-Sudan Archaeological Project – Fourth Cataract: Preliminary Investigation of a Recently Discovered Fort in the ASU BONE Concession near el-Qinifab, Sudan', *Sudan and Nubia*, XXI (2017), pp. 169–76

Bard, Kathryn A., Rodolfo Fattovich, Andrea Manzo and Cinzia Perlingieri, 'Aksum Origins, Kassala and Upper Nubia: New Evidence from Bieta Giyorgis, Aksum', *Archéologie du Nil Moyen*, IX (2002), pp. 31–42

Bennett, Chris, 'Queen Karimala, Daughter of Osochor?', *Göttinger Miszellen*, CLXXIII (1999), pp. 7–8

Binder, Michaela, Neal Spencer and Marie Millet, 'Cemetery D at Amara West: The Ramesside Period and Its Aftermath', *Sudan and Nubia*, XIV (2010), pp. 25–44

Bonnet, Charles, 'Excavations at the Nubian Royal Town of Kerma: 1975–91', *Antiquity*, LXVI (1992), pp. 611–25

——, *The Black Kingdom of the Nile* (Cambridge, MA, and London, 2019)

——, and Dominique Valbelle, *The Nubian Pharaohs: Black Kings on the Nile* (Cairo, 2006)

——, Jacques Reinold, Brigitte Gratien, Bruno Marcolongo and Nicola Surian, 'Les fouilles archéologiques de Kerma (Soudan): Rapport préliminaire sur les campagnes de 1991–1992 et de 1992–1993', *Genava*, XLI (1993), pp. 1–33

Breasted, James Henry, *Ancient Records of Egypt*, vol. I: *The First through the Seventeenth Dynasties* (Chicago, IL, 1906)

Budka, Julia, 'The Early New Kingdom at Sai Island: Preliminary Results Based on the Pottery Analysis (4th Season 2010)', *Sudan and Nubia*, XV (2011), pp. 23–33

——, and Florence Doyen, 'Life in New Kingdom Towns in Upper Nubia: New Evidence from Recent Excavations on Sai Island', *Ägypten und Levante/Egypt and the Levant*, XXII–XXIII (2012/13), pp. 167–208

Burckhardt, John Lewis, *Travels in Nubia*, 2nd edn (New York, 1978)

Burstein, Stanley, 'Rome and Kush: A New Interpretation', in *Nubian Studies 1998: Proceedings of the Ninth Conference of the International Society of Nubian Studies*, ed. Timothy Kendall (Boston, MA, 2004), pp. 14–23

Buzon, Michele, Stuart Tyson Smith and Antonio Simonetti, 'Entanglement and the Formation of the Ancient Nubian Napatan State', *American Anthropologist*, CXVIII/2 (2016), pp. 284–300

Chaix, Louis, 'New Data about Rural Economy in the Kerma Culture: The Site of Gism-el-Arba (Sudan)', *Studies in African Archaeology*, IX (2007), pp. 25–38

Ciampini, Emanuele M., and Grażyna Bąkowska-Czerner, 'Meroitic Kingship and Water: The Case of Napata (B2200)', in *The Fourth Cataract and Beyond: Proceedings of the Twelfth International Conference for Nubian Studies*, ed. Julie R. Anderson and Derek A. Welsby (Leuven, 2014), pp. 695–701

Connah, Graham, *African Civilizations* (Cambridge, 1987)

Cooper, Julien, 'Reconsidering the Location of Yam', *Journal of the American Research Center in Egypt*, XLVIII (2012), pp. 1–21

——, 'Toponymic Strata in Ancient Nubia until the Common Era', *Dowato*, IV (2017), pp. 197–212

D'Ercole, Giulia, 'Seventy Years of Pottery Studies in the Archaeology of Mesolithic and Neolithic Sudan', *African Archaeological Review*, XXXVIII (2021), pp. 345–72

Dafaalla, Samia, 'Succession in the Kingdom of Napata, 900–300 B.C.', *International Journal of African Historical Studies*, XXVI (1993), pp. 167–74

Darnell, John Coleman, *The Inscription of Queen Katimala at Semna: Textual Evidence for the Origins of the Napatan State* (New Haven, CT, and London, 2006)

Davies, Vivian, 'Kush in Egypt: A New Historical Inscription', *Sudan and Nubia*, VII (2003), pp. 52–4

De Garis Davies, Nina, and Alan H. Gardiner, *The Tomb of Huy: Viceroy of Nubia in the Reign of Tut'ankhamūn (No. 40)* (London, 1926)

Dixon, D. M., 'The Land of Yam', *Journal of Egyptian Archaeology*, XLIV (1958), pp. 40–55

Doll, Susan Kay, 'Texts and Decoration on the Napatan Sarcophagi of Anlamani and Aspelta', PhD thesis, Brandeis University, 1978

Doret, Eric, 'Ankhtifi and the Description of his Tomb at Mo'alla', in *For His Ka: Essays Offered in Memory of Klaus Baer*, ed. David P. Silverman (Chicago, IL, 1994), pp. 79–86

Doxey, Denise M., Rita E. Freed and Lawrence M. Berman, *Arts of Ancient Nubia* (Boston, MA, 2018)

Doyen, Florence, 'The New Kingdom Town on Sai Island (Northern Sudan)', *Sudan and Nubia*, XIII (2009), pp. 17–20

——, 'Sai Island New Kingdom Town (Northern Sudan): 3rd and 4th Seasons (2009–2010)', in *The Fourth Cataract and Beyond: Proceedings of the Twelfth International Conference for Nubian Studies*, ed. Julie R. Anderson and Derek A. Welsby (Leuven, 2014), pp. 367–76

Edel, Elmar, 'Inscriften des Alten Reiches XI: Nachtrage zu den Reiseberichten des Hrw-xwif', *Zeitschrift für ägyptische Sprache und Altertumskunde*, LXXXV (1960), pp. 18–23

Edwards, David N., *The Nubian Past: An Archaeology of the Sudan* (Abingdon and New York, 2004)

Eide, Tormod, Tomas Hägg, Richard Holton Pierce and László Török, eds, *Fontes Historiae Nubiorum: Textual Sources for the History of the Middle Nile Region Between the Eighth Century BC and the Sixth Century AD*, 3 vols (Bergen, 1994–8)

Emberling, Geoff, 'Ethnicity in Complex Societies: Archaeological Perspectives', *Journal of Archaeological Research*, V (1997), pp. 295–344

Fattovich, Rodolfo, 'The Problem of Sudanese–Ethiopian Contacts in Antiquity: Status Quaestionis and Current Trends of Research', in *Nubian Studies: Proceedings of the Symposium for Nubian Studies, Selwyn College, Cambridge, 1978*, ed. J. Martin Plumley (Warminster, 1982), pp. 76–86

——, 'At the Periphery of the Empire: The Gash Delta (Eastern Sudan)', in *Egypt and Africa: Nubia from Prehistory to Islam*, ed. W. V. Davies (London, 1991), pp. 40–47

——, 'The Development of Ancient States in the Northern Horn of Africa, *c.* 3000 BC–AD 1000: An Archaeological Outline', *Journal of World Prehistory*, XXIII (2010), pp. 145–75

Fisher, Marjorie M., Peter Lacovara, Salima Ikram and Sue D'Auria, eds, *Ancient Nubia: African Kingdoms on the Nile* (New York and Cairo, 2012)

Friedman, Renée, Margaret Judd and Joel D. Irish, 'The Nubian Cemetery at Hierakonpolis, Egypt: Results of the 2007 Season', *Sudan and Nubia*, XI (2007), pp. 57–71

Gardiner, Alan, 'The Coronation of King Haremhab', *Journal of Egyptian Archaeology*, XXXIX (1953), pp. 13–31

Garstang, John, and A. H. Sayce, 'Second Interim Report on the Excavations at Meroe in Ethiopia', *Liverpool Annals of Archaeology and Anthropology*, IV (1912), pp. 45–71

——, W. J. Phythian-Adams and A. H. Sayce, 'Fifth Interim Report on the Excavations at Meroë in Ethiopia', *Liverpool Annals of Archaeology and Anthropology*, VII (1914–16), pp. 1–24

Gatto, Maria Carmela, 'The Nubian A-Group: A Reassessment', *Archéonil*, XVI (2006), pp. 61–76

Gervers, Michael, 'Cotton and Cotton Weaving in Meroitic Nubia and Medieval Ethiopia', *Textile History*, XXI/1 (1990), pp. 13–30

Gratien, Brigitte, 'Some Rural Settlements at Gism el-Arba in the Northern Dongola Reach', *Sudan and Nubia*, III (1999), pp. 10–12

——, 'L'Habitat 2 de Gism el-Arba: Rapport préliminaire sur un centre de stockage Kerma?', *Cahier de Recherches de l'Institut de Papyrologie et d'Egyptologie de Lille*, XXIII (2003), pp. 29–43

Haaland, Gunnar, and Randi Haaland, 'God of War, Worldly Ruler, and Craft Specialists in the Meroitic Kingdom of Sudan: Inferring Social Identity from Material Remains', *Journal of Social Archaeology*, VII/3 (2007), pp. 372–92

Haaland, Randi, 'Iron Working in an Indian Ocean Context', in *World of Iron*, ed. Jane Humphris and Thilo Rehren (London, 2013), pp. 146–55

Habachi, Labib, *The Second Stela of Kamose and His Struggle against the Hyksos Ruler and His Capital* (Glückstadt, 1972)

Holt, P. M., and M. W. Daly, *A History of the Sudan: From the Coming of Islam to the Present Day*, 5th edn (London, 2000)

Honegger, Matthieu, 'Kerma: L'agglomération pré-Kerma', *Genava*, XLV (1997), pp. 113–18

——, 'The Pre-Kerma Settlement: New Elements Throw Light on the Rise of the First Nubian Kingdom', in *Nubian Studies 1998: Proceedings of the Ninth Conference of the International Society of Nubian Studies*, ed. Timothy Kendall (Boston, MA, 2004), pp. 83–94

——, and Camille Fallet, 'Archers' Tombs of Kerma Ancien', *Kerma: Documents de la mission archéologique suisse au Soudan*, VI (2015), pp. 16–30

Humphris, Jane, Michael F. Charlton, Jake Keen, Lee Sauder and Fareed Alshishani, 'Iron Smelting in Sudan: Experimental Archaeology at the Royal City of Meroe', *Journal of Field Archaeology*, XLIII/5 (2018), pp. 399–416

Jaafari, Shirin, 'Here's the Story behind the Iconic Sudanese Woman in White', *The World*, 10 April 2019, https://theworld.org, accessed 1 September 2021

Kahn, Dan'el, 'The Queen Mother in the Kingdom of Kush: Status, Power and Cultic Role', in *Teshura Le-Zafrira: Studies in the Bible, the History of Israel and the Ancient Near East Presented to Zafrira Ben-Barak*, ed. Mayer I. Gruber et al. (Beer Sheva, 2012), pp. 61–8

Kendall, Timothy, ed., *Nubian Studies 1998: Proceedings of the Ninth Conference of the International Society of Nubian Studies* (Boston, MA, 2004)

——, 'Why Did Taharqa Build His Tomb at Nuri?', in *Between the Cataracts: Proceedings of the 11th Conference for Nubian Studies, Part One: Main Papers*, ed. Włodzimierz Godlewski and Adam Łajtar, Polish Archaeology in the Mediterranean, Supplement Series 2:1 (Warsaw, 2008), pp. 117–47

Kirwan, Laurence P., 'A Survey of Nubian Origins', *Sudan Notes and Records*, XX/1 (1937), pp. 47–62

Kitchen, Kenneth A., *The Third Intermediate Period in Egypt (1100–650 BC)* (Oxford, 2004)

Klemm, Dietrich D., Rosemarie Klemm and Andreas Murr, 'Ancient Gold Mining in the Eastern Desert of Egypt and the Nubian Desert of Sudan', in *Egypt and Nubia: Gifts of the Desert*, ed. Renée Friedman (London, 2002), pp. 215–31

Kormysheva, Eleonora Y., 'On the Origin and Evolution of the Amun Cult in Nubia', in *Nubian Studies 1998: Proceedings of the Ninth Conference of the International Society of Nubian Studies*, ed. Timothy Kendall (Boston, MA, 2004), pp. 109–33

Kraemer, Bryan, and Kate Liszka, 'Evidence for Administration of the Nubian Fortresses in the Late Middle Kingdom: The Semna Dispatches', *Journal of Egyptian History*, IX/1 (2016), pp. 1–65

Leonard, Horace, trans., *The Geography of Strabo* (Cambridge, MA, 1967)

Liszka, Kate, and Bryan Kraemer, 'Evidence for Administration of the Nubian Fortresses in the Late Middle Kingdom: P. Ramesseum 18', *Journal of Egyptian History*, IX/2 (2016), pp. 151–208

Lobban, Richard, 'Greeks, Nubians and Mapping the Ancient Nile', in *Nubian Studies 1998: Proceedings of the Ninth Conference of the International Society of Nubian Studies*, ed. Timothy Kendall (Boston, MA, 2004), pp. 341–8

Lohwasser, Angelika, 'Queenship in Kush: Status, Role and Ideology of Royal Women', *Journal of the American Research Center in Egypt*, XXXVIII (2001), pp. 61–76

——, *The Kushite Cemetery of Sanam: A Non-Royal Burial Ground of the Nubian Capital, c. 800–600 BC* (London, 2010)

——, 'Neujahr in Nubien', in *Ein Forscherleben zwischen den Welten: Zum 80. Geburtstag von Steffen Wenig*, ed. Angelika Lohwasser and Pawel Wolf (Berlin, 2014), pp. 229–36

Manzo, Andrea, 'Apedemak and Dionysos: Further Remarks on the "Cult of the Grape" in Kush', *Sudan and Nubia*, X (2006), pp. 82–94

Markowitz, Yvonne M., and Peter Lacovara, 'The Ferlini Treasure in Archaeological Perspective', *Journal of the American Research Center in Egypt*, XXXIII (1996), pp. 1–9

Minor, Elizabeth, 'The Use of Egyptian and Egyptianizing Material Culture in Nubian Burials of the Classic Kerma Period', PhD thesis, University of California, Berkeley, 2012

——, 'The Use of Egyptian and Egyptianizing Material Culture in Classic Kerma Burials: Winged Sun Discs', in *Les produits de luxe au Proche-Orient ancien, aux âges du Bronze et du Fer*, ed. Michèle Casanova and Martin Feldman (Paris, 2014), pp. 225–34

——, 'Decolonizing Reisner: A Case Study of a Classic Kerma Female Burial for Reinterpreting Early Nubian Archaeological Collections through Digital Archival Resources', in *Nubian Archaeology in the XXIst Century: Proceedings of the Thirteenth International Conference for Nubian Studies* (Leuven, 2018), pp. 251–62

——, 'One More for the Road: Beer, Sacrifice and Commemoration in Ancient Nubian Burials of the Classic Kerma Period', in *Current Research in Egyptology 2017: Proceedings of the Eighteenth Annual Symposium*, ed. Ilaria Incordino et al. (Oxford, 2018), pp. 126–38

Morkot, Robert, *The Black Pharaohs: Egypt's Nubian Rulers* (London, 2000)

——, 'From Conquered to Conquerer: The Organization of Nubia in the New Kingdom and the Kushite Administration of Egypt', in *Ancient Egyptian Administration*, ed. Juan Carlos Moreno García (Leiden, 2013), pp. 911–63

O'Connor, David, 'New Kingdom and Third Intermediate Period, 1552–664 BC', in Bruce G. Trigger, Barry J. Kemp, David O'Connor and Alan B. Lloyd, *Ancient Egypt: A Social History* (Cambridge, 1983), pp. 183–278

——, 'The Locations of Yam and Kush and Their Historical Implications', *Journal of the American Research Center in Egypt*, XXIII (1986), pp. 27–50

——, 'City and Palace in New Kingdom Egypt', *Cahiers de Recherches de l'Institut de Papyrologie et d'Egyptologie de Lille*, XI (1989), pp. 73–87

——, 'Beloved of Maat, the Horizon of Re: The Royal Palace in New Kingdom Egypt', in *Ancient Egyptian Kingship*, ed. David O'Connor and David P. Silverman (Leiden, 1995), pp. 263–300

Okafor, Edwin E., 'New Evidence on Early Iron-Smelting from Southwestern Nigeria', in *The Archaeology of Africa: Food, Metals and Towns*, ed. Thurstan Shaw, Paul Sinclair, Bassey Andah and Alex Okpoko (London and New York, 1993), pp. 432–48

Pagliari, Giulia, 'Function and Significance of Ancient Egyptian Royal Palaces from the Middle Kingdom to the Saite Period', PhD thesis, University of Birmingham and La 'Sapienza', University of Rome, 2012

Parkinson, Richard B., and Neal Spencer, 'The *Teaching of Amenemhat* at Amara West', *Egyptian Archaeology*, XXXV (2009), pp. 25–7

Phillipson, David W., *African Archaeology*, 3rd edn (Cambridge, 2005)

Poggo, Scopas, 'The Origins and Culture of Blacksmiths in Kuku Society of the Sudan, 1797–1955', *Journal of African Cultural Studies*, XVIII/2 (2006), pp. 169–86

Pope, Jeremy, *The Double Kingdom under Taharqo: Studies in the History of Kush and Egypt, c. 690–664 BC* (Leiden, 2014)

Powell, Eric A., 'Miniature Pyramids of Sudan', *Archaeology*, LXVI/4 (2013), pp. 30–34

Reimer, Thomas O., 'The Presentation of Gold in the Reliefs of the Eastern Staircase of the Apadana in Persepolis', *Iranian Journal of Archaeological Studies*, III (2013), pp. 57–63

Reisner, George Andrew, *Excavations at Kerma: Joint Egyptian Expedition of Harvard University and the Boston Museum of Fine Arts*, 2 vols (Cambridge, MA, 1923)

Revez, Jean, 'The Metaphorical Use of the Kinship Term *sn* "Brother"', *Journal of the American Research Center in Egypt*, XL (2003), pp. 123–31

Rilly, Claude, 'Meroitische Texte aus Naga/ Meroitic Texts from Naga', in *Königsstadt Naga: Grabungen in der Wüste des Sudan/ Naga-Royal City: Excavations in the Desert of the Sudan*, ed. Karla Kröper, Sylvia Schoske and Dietrich Wildung (Munich and Berlin, 2011), pp. 176–201

——, and Alex de Voogt, *The Meroitic Language and Writing System* (Cambridge, 2012)

Roccati, Alessando, 'L'Hellénisme dans l'architecture et la décoration des palais de Napata', in *Méroé: Un Empire sur le Nil*, ed. Michel Baud (Paris, 2010), pp. 95–6

Rocheleau, Caroline M., *Amun Temples in Nubia: A Typological Study of New Kingdom, Napatan and Meroitic Temples* (Oxford, 2008)

Sackho-Autissier, Aminata, 'La Guerre entre Méroé et Rome, 25–21 av. J.-C.', in *Méroé: Un Empireire sur le Nil*, ed. Michel Baud (Paris, 2010), p. 73

Schellinger, Sarah M., 'Victory Stela of Pianki', in *Milestone Documents*, ed. Brian Bonhomme (Dallas, TX, 2014), pp. 91–107

Simpson, William Kelly, ed., *The Literature of Ancient Egypt: An Anthology of Stories, Instructions, Stelae, Autobiographies, and Poetry*, 3rd edn (New Haven, CT, and London, 2003)

Sist, Loredana, 'Motivi ellenistici nell'architettura meroitica: nuove scoperte a Napata', in *Acta Nubica: Proceedings of the X International Conference of Nubian Studies*, ed. Isabella Caneva and Alessandro Roccati (Rome, 2006), pp. 475–81

Smith, Stuart Tyson, 'Askut and the Role of the Second Cataract Forts', *Journal of the American Research Center in Egypt*, XXVIII (1991), pp. 107–32

——, *Wretched Kush: Ethnic Identities and Boundaries in Egypt's Nubian Empire* (New York, 2003)

Somaglino, Claire, and Pierre Tallet, 'Gebel Sheikh Suleiman: A First Dynasty Relief after All . . .', *Archéonil*, XXV (2015), pp. 123–34

Spence, Kate, and Pamela Rose, 'Fieldwork at Sesebi, 2010', in *The Fourth Cataract and Beyond: Proceedings of the Twelfth International Conference for Nubian Studies*, ed. Julie R. Anderson and Derek A. Welsby (Leuven, 2014), pp. 409–15

——, et al., 'Fieldwork at Sesebi, 2009', *Sudan and Nubia*, XIII (2009), pp. 38–46

——, et al., 'Sesebi 2011', *Sudan and Nubia*, XV (2011), pp. 34–8

Spencer, Neal, 'Cemeteries and a Late Ramesside Suburb at Amara West', *Sudan and Nubia*, XIII (2009), pp. 47–60

——, 'Amara West: Considerations on Urban Life in Colonial Kush', in *The Fourth Cataract and Beyond: Proceedings of the Twelfth International Conference for Nubian Studies*, ed. Julie R. Anderson and Derek A. Welsby (Leuven, 2014), pp. 457–85

——, Anna Stevens and Michaela Binder, *Amara West: Living in Egyptian Nubia* (London, 2014)

Strudwick, Nigel C., *Texts from the Pyramid Age* (Atlanta, GA, 2005)

Török, László, 'Ambulatory Kingship and Settlement History: A Study on the Contribution of Archaeology to Meroitic History', in *Études nubiennes: Conférence de Genève; Actes du VIIe Congrès international d'études nubiennes*, ed. Charles Bonnet (Geneva, 1992), pp. 111–26

——, *Birth of an Ancient African Kingdom: Kush and Her Myth of the State in the First Millennium BC* (Lille, 1995)

——, *The Kingdom of Kush: Handbook of the Napatan-Meroitic Civilization* (Leiden, 1997)

——, *The Image of the Ordered World in Ancient Nubian Art: The Construction of the Kushite Mind (800 BC–300 AD)* (Leiden, 2002)

——, 'Space, Temple, and Society: On the Built Worldview of the Twenty-Fifth Dynasty in Nubia', in *Acta Nubica: Proceedings of the X International Conference of Nubian Studies*, ed. Isabella Caneva and Alessandro Roccati (Rome, 2006), pp. 231–8

——, *Between Two Worlds: The Frontier Region between Ancient Nubia and Egypt, 3700 BC–500 AD* (Leiden, 2009)

——, *Hellenizing Art in Ancient Nubia, 300 BC–AD 250, and Its Egyptian Models: A Study in 'Acculturation'* (Leiden, 2011)

——, with I. Hofmann and I. Nagy, *Meroe City: An Ancient African Capital; John Garstang's Excavations in Sudan*, 2 vols (London, 1997)

Trigger, Bruce G., *History and Settlement in Lower Nubia* (New Haven, CT, 1965)

Van Pelt, W. Paul, 'Revising Egypto-Nubian Relations in New Kingdom Lower Nubia: From Egyptianization to Cultural Entanglement', *Cambridge Archaeological Journal*, XXIII/3 (2013), pp. 523–50

Vercoutter, Jean, 'Un Palais des "Candaces", contemporain d'Auguste (Fouilles à Wad-ban-Naga 1958–1960)', *Syria*, XXXIX (1962), pp. 263–99

Vincentelli, Irene, *Hillat el-Arab: The Joint Sudanese–Italian Expedition in the Napatan Region, Sudan* (Oxford, 2006)

Vrtal, Vlastimil, 'The Palace of Queen Amanishakheto (WBN 100)', in *Wad Ben Naga: 1821–2013*, ed. Pavel Onderka et al. (Prague, 2013), pp. 57–62

Welsby, Derek, *The Kingdom of Kush: The Napatan and Meroitic Empires* (London, 1996)

——, 'Excavations at Kawa, 2009–10', *Sudan and Nubia*, XIV (2010), pp. 48–55

——, and Julie R. Anderson, eds, *Sudan Ancient Treasures: Recent Discoveries from the Sudan National Museum*, exh. cat., British Museum (London, 2004)

Williams, Bruce Beyer, *Excavations between Abu Simbel and the Sudan Frontier*, vol. III: *The A-Group Royal Cemetery at Qustul: Cemetery L* (Chicago, IL, 1986)

Wolf, Pawel, 'Essay über den meroitischen Eklektizismus in Musawwarat es Sufra, oder: Woher stammt der meroitische Einraumtempel?', in *Ein Forscherleben zwischen den Welten: Zum 80. Geburtstag von Steffen Wenig*, ed. Angelika Lohwasser and Pawel Wolf (Berlin, 2014), pp. 351–94

——, and Claude Rilly, 'Les Stèles de Hamadab', in *Méroé: Un Empire sur le Nil*, ed. Michel Baud (Paris, 2010), pp. 160–61

Yellin, Janice, 'The Role of Anubis in Meroitic Religion', in *Nubian Studies: Proceedings of the Symposium for Nubian Studies 1978*, ed. J. M. Plumley (Warminster, 1982), pp. 227–34

——, 'Egyptian Religion and Its Ongoing Impact on the Formation of the Napatan State. A Contribution to László Török's Main Paper: The Emergence of the Kingdom of Kush and her Myth of the State in the First Millennium BC', *Cahiers de Recherches de l'Institut de Papyrologie et d'Egyptologie de Lille*, XVII/1 (1995), pp. 243–63

——, 'The Chronology and Attribution of Royal Pyramids at Meroe and Gebel Barkal: Beg N 8, Beg N 12, Bar 5 and Bar 2', *Journal of Ancient Egyptian Interconnections*, VI/1 (2014), pp. 76–88

——, 'The Kushite Nature of Early Meroitic Mortuary Religion: A Pragmatic Approach to Osirian Beliefs', in *Ein Forscherleben zwischen den Welten: Zum 80. Geburtstag von Steffen Wenig*, ed. Angelika Lohwasser and Pawel Wolf (Berlin, 2014), pp. 395–404

Yoyotte, Jean, 'Pour une localization du pays de Iam', *Bulletin de l'Institut Français d'Archéologie Orientale*, LII (1953), pp. 173–8

Żurawski, Bogdan, 'Pliny's "Tergedum" Discovered', *Sudan and Nubia*, II (1998), pp. 74–81

——, 'Dongola Reach: The Southern Dongola Reach Survey, 1998/1999', *Polish Archaeology in the Mediterranean*, XI (2000), pp. 209–21

ACKNOWLEDGEMENTS

This book would not have been possible without the support and guidance of friends near and far, especially Denise Doxey, Stacy Davidson, Christina Burke Mathison, Aleksandra Ksiezak and Elizabeth Minor. Particular thanks go to Ahmed El-Ameen Ahmed El-Hassan (Sokhari) for his assistance with images from the Sudan National Museum. Thanks also to Dave Watkins and Amy Salter at Reaktion Books for their patience and guidance throughout this process. And, of course, to my parents, Nan and Rich, for their endless love and support.

PHOTO ACKNOWLEDGEMENTS

The author and publishers wish to express their thanks to the below sources of illustrative material and/or permission to reproduce it:

The J. Paul Getty Museum, Los Angeles: p. 17; drawn by Aleksandra Ksiezak, after C. M. Firth, *The Archæological Survey of Nubia: Report for 1910–1911* (Cairo, 1927): p. 37; drawn by Aleksandra Ksiezak, after N.-C. Grimal, *La stèle triomphale de Pi('ankhy) au Musée du Caire: JE 48862 et 47086–47089* (Cairo, 1981): p. 78; drawn by Aleksandra Ksiezak, after N.-C. Grimal, *Quatre stèles napatéenes au Musée du Cairo: JE 48863–48866* (Cairo, 1981): p. 126; drawn by Aleksandra Ksiezak, after Claire Somaglino and Pierre Tallet, 'Gebel Sheikh Suleiman: A First Dynasty Relief after All . . .', *Archéo-Nil*, XXV (2015): p. 38; from R. Lepsius, *Denkmäler aus Ägypten und Äthiopien: Nach den Zeichnungen der von seiner Majestät dem Könige von Preussen Friedrich Wilhelm IV nach diesen Ländern gesendeten und in den Jahren 1842–1845 ausgeführten wissenschaftlichen Expedition auf Befehl seiner Majestät*, vol. V (Berlin, 1855), photo the New York Public Library: p. 133; The Metropolitan Museum of Art, New York: pp. 41, 53, 64, 85, 102, 111; © Mission archéologique suisse-franco-soudanaise de Kerma-Doukki Gel: pp. 48, 52; photos © 2022 Museum of Fine Arts, Boston: pp. 12, 16, 36, 49, 57, 60, 61, 73, 80; photo Carole Raddato (CC BY-SA 2.0): p. 72; photos Sarah M. Schellinger: pp. 45, 81, 89, 92, 93, 103, 113, 114, 128, 139, 140; Sudan National Museum, Khartoum: pp. 33 (no. 26883), 69 (no. 63/4/5), 149 (no. 15309); © The Trustees of the British Museum: pp. 39, 99, 131, 145 (map by Claire Thorne); © UNESCO (CC BY-SA 3.0 IGO): p. 21; The Walters Art Museum, Baltimore, MD: p. 98; courtesy of the Wendorf Archive, the British Museum: p. 32.

꩜ INDEX